Battleground Europe
GUILLEMONT

Battleground Europe

GUILLEMONT

Michael Stedman

Series editor
Nigel Cave

Pen & Sword
MILITARY

This book is dedicated to the memory of the numberless soldiers who fought on both sides of the terrible divide and whose graves lie in profligate waste at Guillemont, unmarked and unknown. In particular I should like to recall the life of one such young subaltern, 2nd Lieutenant John Hayes (Jack) Fearnhead, who was twenty one years old when he succumbed to wounds on 13 August 1916. I should have liked to have met him in his old age. Jack was an effervescent and delightful character whose memory is still recalled with great affection by his family. He served in the 1/7th Battalion, the King's (Liverpool) Regiment.

First published in Great Britain in 1998 by Leo Cooper
Reprinted in 2012 by
PEN & SWORD MILITARY
An imprint of
Pen & Sword Books Ltd
47 Church Street
Barnsley
South Yorkshire
S70 2AS

Copyright © Michael Stedman, 1998, 2012

ISBN 978 0 85052 591 5

The right of Michael Stedman to be identified as Author
of this work has been asserted by him in accordance with the
Copyright, Designs and Patents Act 1988.

A CIP catalogue record for this book is available from the British Library

Printed and bound in England
By CPI Group (UK) Ltd, Croydon, CR0 4YY

Pen & Sword Books Ltd incorporates the Imprints of Pen & Sword Aviation,
Pen & Sword Family History, Pen & Sword Maritime, Pen & Sword Military,
Pen & Sword Discovery, Wharncliffe Local History, Wharncliffe True Crime,
Wharncliffe Transport, Pen & Sword Select, Pen & Sword Military Classics,
Leo Cooper, The Praetorian Press, Remember When,
Seaforth Publishing and Frontline Publishing

For a complete list of Pen & Sword titles please contact
PEN & SWORD BOOKS LIMITED
47 Church Street, Barnsley, South Yorkshire, S70 2AS, England
E-mail: enquiries@pen-and-sword.co.uk
Website: www.pen-and-sword.co.uk

CONTENTS

Jack Fearnhead's life before the onset of war had been carefree and happy, within the security of a close and loving family. There were two sisters and he was the youngest of four brothers. This photograph shows Jack with his parents and younger sister. [Hall]

Introduction by Series Editor

This latest volume in the Battleground Europe series is centred around the village of Guillemont. To go there now it is impossible to envisage the ghastly image that men like Fr Willy Doyle, Ernst Junger and the Master of Belhaven tried to describe in words. Now it is an utterly placid agricultural community, where the loudest noise is the barking of farmyard dogs and, in season, the sounds of shot guns echoing across the fields. It is no exaggeration to say that most of the traffic for a good proportion of the year consists of British vehicles engaged in a pilgrimage to these terrible killing fields. How can one replace this scene with the sights, smells and fearsome sounds of hundreds of guns, trench mortars, machine guns and the tortured wounded; of the decomposing bodies of seemingly uncountable soldiers, their stench and mangled limbs – all in all a vista of desolation and despair? The answer for most, if not all of us, is that it is impossible, and beyond our imaginative capabilities, which is just as well.

The book follows on from the comparative success that was gained in this sector, the southernmost part of the 1 July battlefield, by British troops, working in immediate conjunction with their French allies. Various features of the ground, such as Trones Wood and the village itself, were vital to the success of further, and larger, operations close by, such as the Dawn Attack on 14 July and the push using tanks for the first time on 15 September. It is the story of a struggle without any form of glamour; a large number of small (by the standards of the Great War) attacks, often hastily contrived against a determined and resolute enemy defending extraordinarily well prepared positions. There were numerous examples of great heroism, perhaps most famously amongst them being the actions of Noel Chavasse, which were to win him the first of his Victoria Crosses.

But the events at and around Guillemont during the summer and autumn of 1916 are characteristic of much that happened in what is now collectively known as the Battle of the Somme 1916. It became, for the British, their first great grinding down battle which was then followed by an almost unending series of similar battles that culminated in the Armistice of November 1918. It destroyed the naïve enthusiasm that was the hallmark of many of the New Army divisions that set off with such confidence on 1 July, and replaced it with a resigned and dogged determination that ultimately resulted in an enormously expensive victory. This great battle also cost the German fighting machine much – it destroyed what remained of the great field army that was mobilised in August 1914. By the end of it all, brought to a halt by the onset of winter, both armies had become fully conversant with the concept – and reality –

Opposite: The 16th (Irish) Division's memorial is unveiled in Guillemont in the 20s.

of that doom-laden word, attrition. Falkenhayn had been the first to preach its military possibilities when he put forward his scheme for Verdun (though neglecting to tell his Army commander that this was what he had in mind); Haig realised that this was what the war was coming to. It has become a word synonymous with the heartlessness of generals; yet it also means the destruction of the enemy's will (and ability) to fight. In the context of the time, it is difficult to see how the war was to be won by other means, and given that the war was one that not only had to be fought but also had to be won, as very great issues were at stake, it is difficult to see how else things could be done, certainly at this stage of the war.

What cannot be denied is that the detail was more often than not poorly planned and poorly executed even allowing for the considerable practical difficulties that faced all levels of command. This book, by its nature, concerns itself with the detail involved in this relatively tiny part of the Western Front – of monumental significance to the men who were here, part of a jigsaw to those who oversaw the operation. Thus this book – and others in the series – do not try and explain the why, except possibly in the broadest sense, but the who and the where and the how. Since this is the way that most of those who fought and were wounded or died or were shattered here saw things, it has both value and immediacy – but readers should be prepared to read further and deeper if they want to understand more fully the great tragedy that was the Great War.

Nigel Cave
Ely Place, London.

Author's introduction

The history of the Great War is very much the people's history, a story with which we feel affinity because the documentation and familial stories are so readily accessible to us all. In this context a thought which has constantly engaged me whilst writing this small volume is the enormous number of infantry and supporting units which were drawn into the battles for Trones Wood and Guillemont. Of course, that was equally true of both sides whose men fought here. It therefore proved impossible to name anything other than a proportion of those myriad battalions who came and were swallowed, their men fixed forever into the terrible black hole which Guillemont became. The omission of any regiments from the narrative is therefore in no way suggestive that its contribution had little or no significance. But sadly, to attempt the inclusion of every unit into the story would have made this book, in the limited space available, little more than a list of participants. Instead I have sought to make clear the tactical and topographical factors which made Guillemont such a terrible and unforgettable place in the summer and autumn of 1916, illustrating that with what I hope are representative and illuminating contemporary accounts.

Michael Stedman.
Leigh, Worcester.

Acknowledgements

Within the narrative record of events here at Bernafay and Trones Woods and Guillemont I have made considerable use of many words, often penned in haste amidst terrible danger more than eighty years ago. To all of the soldiers who wrote at that time and those who penned their memoirs during the post war era I am grateful and can only stand in awe. However, it would have been impossible to complete this guide without the help of many of my contemporaries. In particular I should like to thank Nigel Cave who made a number of very helpful suggestions as to sources and who, as always, has undertaken a thorough review of this work; Derek Butler and other staff of the Commonwealth War Graves Commission at Maidenhead, John Baker of The Map Shop in Upton-upon-Severn who kindly supplied a number of IGN maps; Geoff Thomas who has walked many miles of the Somme battlefield in all sorts of weather with me and in whose company the sun has always seemed to shine kindly. Sue Cox. Elsie Davis. John Garwood. Pam Hall. Jennifer Hartley. Simon Jones and the Trustees of the National Museums & Galleries on Merseyside – King's Regiment Collection for permission to use the photograph of Sergeant Jones, V.C., Lieutenant Colonel Tony Moore of the King's Regiment and Barrie Thorpe who is the Memorials Officer for the Western Front Association. Ralph Whitehead. The Mayor of Guillemont, Monsieur Dazin. Paul Reed has been generous in providing a number of interesting contemporary photographs which appear within this guide. The staff at the Public Records Office in Kew and the Imperial War Museum have provided me with much help, assistance and considered judgement. Many other members of the Western Front Association have also helped in greatly enhancing my knowledge of the Guillemont area. To all of these people I should like to extend my sincere thanks whilst making clear that any errors which remain within the text are solely of my own making.

Opposite: Stretcher bearers from the 5th Division near Waterlot Farm, 3 to 6 September 1916.

Sensible equipment and advice for visitors

There is nothing like getting outside in the fresh air and walking. Its good exercise, you can do it on your own, with a friend or as one of a large group. During the last decade the growth of interest in the history of the Great War has led to many more organised tours which has added to the pressure which some sites, such as Tyne Cot at Passchendaele or Thiepval here on the Somme, experience. But wherever you are on the Western Front's miles of accessible battlefield history one of the greatest pleasures, and the most salutary and moving of experiences, is to 'walk the course' of an event in the extraordinary history of the Great War. Often the interest lies in reconstructing in our minds the encounters of the men who were there and sharing the chance insights and discoveries with friends. I cannot forget the first time I saw and walked many of these places, the Salford Pals' attack on Thiepval on 1st July 1916, the tragic advance of the Tyneside battalions of the 34th Division at La Boisselle that same day, and following the story of the Manchester Pals here at Trones Wood with my great friend Vincent Sleigh.

But whoever you are following, or whatever you are trying to explain and understand, certain items are always likely to enhance your pleasure. It is worth noting that here the trees of Trones Wood provide admirable shelter. The walks I have described should never take more than two hours. The area south-east of Maricourt is picturesque and attractive. South of the Albert – Peronne road at Vaux, Fargny and Curlu there are wonderful places to laze away an afternoon on the south facing slopes above the river Somme. In the late summer of 1916, for a lucky few who found the time and opportunity to get down here to swill the chalk dust from their aching limbs, this was a haven of tranquillity. Sun cream and plenty of drinks are absolutely essential, especially in hot summer weather. Stout shoes or walking boots at any time of the year are vital. Wellington boots and thick socks in winter or soon after rain are needed, along with appropriate outer clothing. Incidentally, you could attempt to complete the walks in the immediate vicinity of Guillemont in one day. Therefore, for those of you intent on spending just such a full day here 'in the field' and who want to record your visit carefully some further items are advisable. Take a sandwich, a camera, a pen and notebook to record where you took your photographs and perhaps to note your visit in the cemetery registers. A pair of binoculars would be helpful, especially in a location such as Maltz Horn Farm where the views are extensive. However, and finally, a decent penknife with a corkscrew, a first aid kit and a small rucksack capable of carrying everything comfortably should complete your requirements.

Here at Guillemont, as elsewhere on the Somme, a metal detector is, let us be frank, an embarrassment. Many people come here to the fields to sweep for any remnants of clothing, perhaps the occasional Manchester or Liverpool Pals' shoulder title, or whatever. But in my opinion they are better left to rest and await a chance discovery. To be seen digging within sight of what should be places of peace and reflection near to the Guillemont Road Cemetery is almost to desecrate the memory of those whose names are recorded so starkly on those bare white headstones. The spectacle of lone Britons sweeping their electronic plates across empty fields fills me with sadness. This should be a place where a more rewarding and meaningful history reveals itself, without recourse to indignity.

No significant preparation is required to cope with medical requirements. It is however very sensible to ensure that you carry an E111 form which gives reciprocal rights to medical and hospital treatment in France, as well as all other EC countries. The necessary documents can be obtained free from any main post office. As in the UK where you are in a working agricultural area and may be scratched or cut by rusty metals, ensure that your tetanus vaccination is up to date. Comprehensive personal and vehicle insurance is advisable. In this context it is worth noting that there have been a number of thefts from British tourists' vehicles in the area of the Somme, even when parked near to the cemeteries and features around Guillemont. To help arrange and plan your stay I have identified a list of campsites, hotels and B&B accommodation within easy distance of the village in Chapter 1, which deals with the designated area today. However, a fuller guide to the many excellent hotels, restaurants, auberges and overnight accommodations available in the Picardie area can be obtained from the Comite Regional du Tourisme de Picardie, 3 Rue Vincent Auriol - 80000 Amiens - Tel: 00 33 322 91 10 15.

How to use this book

This guide can be used in preparation for your visit, in front of the fire at home on a cold winter evening. In that case it is perhaps best read from start to finish. I think you will have a sound feel for Guillemont at the end of one or two evenings' reading and might be ready to book your cross channel ferry or tunnel for those days in March and April when the weather begins to clear, the fields are ploughed and crop growth has not yet hidden the detail and topography of the ground. But the guide is also designed as a pocket reference, a quick supplement to your knowledge when you are 'walking the course', and need an explanation or clarification.

By far the best way to see the Guillemont area is on foot or bicycle. At the end of the text you can find a number of suggested routes making use of the paths and tracks which are accessible to these means of transport. The two chapters dealing with 1916's historic events within the designated area are obviously in chronological order. Although there was fighting here during 1918 this guide is not intended to cover that conflict in great detail since it will be the subject of a further volume in this series.

I suggest that a tour by car or coach is the best way to get your bearings and to give an overview of the whole area. Again I have suggested a tour to highlight the main features of the area, along roads which are easily accessible. The roads covered on this route are usually quite satisfactory for coaches and involve no dangerous turns through 180°! This tour is to be found at the end of the book and is strongly recommended to those of you not already conversant with the area. It is worth noting that some of the tracks and smaller roads to be found on the IGN maps of the area are not suitable for coaches. Cars without four wheel drive will find difficulty in getting along some minor tracks, for example those leading to and around Bois Favier. You would be most unwise to attempt to drive around or through the confines of Trones Wood in any vehicle, although the track leading along the east of Trones Wood northwards to Longueval is usually accessible! Be prepared to walk is the best advice that I can give, but do take care to lock all valuables, especially cameras and other inviting items, out of sight in the boot of your vehicle.

A lane in front of Guillemont showing the havoc wrought by the British bombardment on the defences, 3 - 4 September 1916.

On the subject of Maps

Unlike two of the previous villages about which I have written in this series, Thiepval and La Boisselle, the village of Guillemont is located firmly within just one IGN 1:25000 series map. That map is numbered 2408 est, Bray-sur-Somme. However, you would also find 2408 ouest, Albert, a useful addition since this covers all of the western approaches to the Guillemont area from the direction of Albert. For general access to the area of the Somme sheet 4 in the 1:100,000 IGN green series, Laon and Arras, is very useful. A compass is also an essential companion. For those of you interested in detail beyond the northern part of this guide Bapaume East and Bapaume West (2407 est et ouest) would also prove to be sensible purchases. Taken together these four maps cover the entirety of the British sector of the 1916 Battle of the Somme. Such maps, and many others covering the area of the Western Front, can be obtained by post from The Map Shop in Upton-upon-Severn (01684 593146) or from Waterstones' Booksellers who maintain another excellent specialist map department in Manchester.

I have identified here the maps which appear within this guide. For most navigational and walking purposes these will be sufficient for your enjoyment of this area. However, for a really intimate knowledge of each location the 1:10,000 and 1:5,000 trench maps are indispensable to the serious student or expert. 1;10,000 maps approximate to a scale of six inches to the mile. In order to gain detailed understanding a trench map is therefore indispensable.

Map 1. **Page 25**. The Trones Wood – Guillemont battlefield area, showing the pre-war geography of the area. This is taken from the 1;40,000 sheets which accompanied the *Official History* volume detailing the fighting leading to the first day of the Battle of the Somme.

Map 2. **Page 28**. The dispositions of XIII Corps' men in the vicinity of Maricourt / Montauban before and after their successful attack on 1 July 1916. Taken from the *Official History* series of maps, 1916 Vol I.

Map 3. **Page 29**. The Objectives allotted to the 7th, 18th and 30th British Divisions along with the French 39th and 11th Divisions for 1 July, taken from the *Official History* series of maps, 1916 Vol I.

Map 4. **Page 31**. The advance made by the French XX Corps (Sixth Army) between Bois Faviere and Curlu on the morning of 1 July 1916. *Official History, 1916* Vol 1.

Map 5. Page 38-39. Taken from the 1:10,000 series trench map, corrected to 2/6/1916, this is a segment of 62.c.NW1 showing the area around the Briqueterie, Hardecourt and Maltz Horn Farm.

Map 6. Page 54. Maxwell's troop dispositions within Trones Wood, 14 July 1916.

Map 7. Page 64. Detail from the 1:10,000 trench map (corrected to 24/7/1916) showing the Trones Wood – Arrow Head Copse – Guillemont area in detail.

Map 8. Page 66. Map issued to 19th Manchester officers showing the first stages of the operations launched against Guillemont by the soldiers of 30th Division at 3.40 am on 23 July.

Map 9. Page 81. Detail from sheet 62cNW1 – 1:10,000 trench map, corrected to 2/6/1916, showing the Maltz Horn Farm – Angle Wood area at the extreme southern end of the British sector of the Somme battlefield.

Map 10. Page 85. The OH Map opposite pp 190, Military Operations France and Belgium 1916, Vol 2.

Map 11. Page 108. Showing the 12th King's at Guillemont's final capture (3 September 1916).

Map 12. Page 115. Detail from the Wedge Wood, Falfemont Farm, Oakhanger Wood and Angle Wood areas, north of Maurepas and south-east of Guillemont, taken from two 1:10,000 trench maps.

Map 13. Page 123. The complex of trenches which existed around the Guillemont Road cemetery in the late summer and autumn of 1916.

Map 14. Page 129. Detail taken from the 1:10,000 trench map, 62cNW1, showing the location of Captain Heumann's grave.

Map 15. Page 136. A General Tour of the Guillemont area.

Map 16. Page 140. The Bernafay Wood walk area.

Map 17. Page 142. The Trones Wood walk area.

Map 18. Page 146. Maricourt, Hardecourt, Maltz Horn area today.

Map 19. Page 147. Detail from 1:10,000 trench map covering the Maricourt, Faviere Wood, Hardecourt, Maltz Horn Farm areas, 1916.

Map 20. Page 150. Detail from the 1:10,000 trench map, dated corrected to 15/8/1916, 57cSW3, showing the captured German positions at Delville Wood (Longueval), north Guillemont and Ginchy.

You should note that the trench maps, which are available from the Imperial War Museum Department of Printed Books (Tel: 0171 416 5348) or the cartographer of the Western Front Association (members only), follow a specific sequence and should be referred to by the numbers usually found in their top right hand corner. Unfortunately the Trones Wood and Guillemont area is covered by two sheets belonging to the 1:10,000 trench map series. Those are sheet 57cSW3, entitled Longueval, which covers the villages of Longueval and Bazentin-le-Petit, Ginchy, Guillemont and Montauban; and sheet 62cNW1, entitled Maricourt, which covers Maltz Horn Farm, Maricourt, Hardecourt-aux-Bois and the area towards the River Somme. Variously dated versions are available from both sources. In the text I have sometimes referred to locations which are noted on such trench maps, but not on present day maps. In such cases I have where necessary given the relevant trench map reference to help you identify the exact position. For example, 'Waterlot Farm' north-east of Trones Wood was located on sheet 57cSW3, at reference S.18.c.9,1.

One feature which the young or first time visitor might wish for is an easily accessible reconstruction which gives an insight into the conditions which prevailed around Guillemont at the height of the conflict. One such source of insight and empathy is to be found at Newfoundland Park, two miles north-west of Thiepval on the Auchonvillers road out of Hamel, the D73. This is an area of preserved battlefield, purchased by the government of Newfoundland after the Great War. Further detailed insight can be obtained at the two quality museums which are within reasonable distance. The first, the Musee des Abris, at Albert below the celebrated Basilica, is only twenty minutes away by car. The second, the Historial, at Peronne, is well worth the longer journey, but you should remember to set aside a good forty minutes travelling time, each way. Take the D938 running south-east from Albert to Peronne, a route which will enable you to follow the southern arm of the British front lines as they existed before the opening of the battle of the Somme.

One extraordinary fact about the Somme and Ancre battlefield is that after the utter devastation of the Great War many of the tracks and other human geographical features were reconstructed in the 1920s with an uncanny similarity to their pre-war locations. Most detail shown on trench maps of the Trones Wood – Guillemont area still stand true today. Initially the processes of reconstruction were almost insurmountably difficult. In order to help, many of the villages were adopted by some of Britain's towns and cities.

However, in the early 1920s, as more villagers returned to rebuild their homes and lives with the reparations monies wrung from Weimar Germany, every effort was made to find the exact location of their pre-war houses. Sometimes, when a villager did not return that plot was left vacant, in many cases still so today! But, we should remember that Guillemont is a working village, a community whose roots are based in centuries of toil on the land which is also our place of interest. This is not open access land on the National Trust model. It is all too easy to let our two interests clash. During the autumn months, in particular, be aware of the numerous shooting parties. The farmers will not welcome the sight of your tramping the fields with little regard to crops and seeds. Please ask before you enter. Please keep to the paths and the edges of each field.

As someone said recently, 'My history but his land!'

Late Autumn 1916 and the onset of rain turns the shell-torn landscape around Guillemont into a quagmire.

Chapter One

OUR DESIGNATED AREA TODAY

Most people visiting the Somme battlefield for the first time join the straight road which runs between Albert and Bapaume, the D929, along which it was planned to execute the 'Big Push'. This road neatly bisects the British sector of the first Battle of the Somme. However, the events which unfolded throughout the morning of the 1st July and on the following days meant that far greater emphasis would subsequently be placed by the British army upon the areas south of the Bapaume road rather than to its north. At the very eastern end of the southern arm of the British battlefront on 1st July lay the villages of Maricourt and Montauban. Here the New Army divisions within XIII Corps of Rawlinson's Fourth Army joined hands with the French soldiers of XX Corps. A short distance to the north-east of Maricourt lies Favier Wood (Bois Favier), which was one of the immediate first day objectives for the French army, and the village of Hardecourt-aux-Bois.[1]

From Hardecourt a road leads north towards the village of

Hardecourt, photographed during its occupation by German troops, before damage wrought by the French artillery bombardments devastated this place in June 1916.

Guillemont. Between Montauban and Guillemont lay two substantial areas of woodland, Bernafay and Trones[2]. These two woods lay between the British army's first day objectives and the main German second position which here ran from outside Longueval, past Waterlot Farm and in front of Guillemont. The first of these woods to be captured by the British was Bernafay Wood. However, the subsequent attempts to capture Trones Wood resulted in far more severe fighting. The origins of that severity lay in the fact that the capture of Trones Wood was seen as an essential precursor before the night attack towards Bazentin, due on the morning of 14th July, could be launched with any degree of confidence in its outcome.

East of Trones Wood the D64 leads past the Guillemont Road Cemetery and into the village of Guillemont. North-west of Guillemont is the forbidding outline of Delville Wood which contains the South African memorial. As you look along the D20 towards the village of Longueval and Delville Wood your line of sight passes Waterlot Farm which is dealt with within this guide. East of the village of Guillemont lies Combles whilst to the north-east Ginchy can be seen, although outside the scope of this guide, only one kilometre away. If you are in search of refreshment on a hot day then Combles has a number of shops and a bar where refreshment can be purchased. However, the most frequently used place to pick up supplies, some

The church and Guillemont village today.

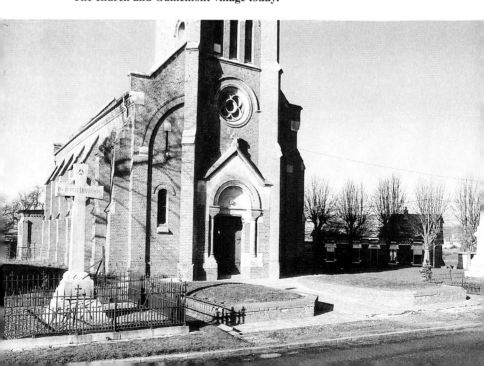

distance to the west, is the town of Albert, familiar to almost every British soldier who served during the first Battle of the Somme. Today Albert describes itself as being only the "3eme Ville de la Somme", but quite properly "la Cite d'Ancre". The Town Hall square in Albert often hosts a market and there are three small supermarkets nearby which can all provide a sound array of food and refreshments.

However, away from the town of Albert, the area south of the Albert – Bapaume road in the quadrant east and north-east of Albert in the direction of Hardecourt and past Pozieres is distinguished by an enormous crescent of substantial woodlands. Having been devastated by shellfire during the Great War these woodlands are, once again, mature and dark, completely dominating the atmosphere and topography of this areas. In almost every case these prominent woods have been allowed to re-establish themselves on exactly the same sites as they occupied before war ravaged the area.

Leaving Albert the village of Guillemont can be reached in a number of ways. Each route has a very different character.

The first and most southerly route is along the D938 Albert to Peronne road. Continue along the D938 until you reach Maricourt which lies on this guide's western boundary. After passing the sites of the Devons and Gordons cemeteries this road begins to rise up as it approaches Maricourt and fine views can be had along the southern arm of the British battlefront on 1st July. At Maricourt, where the British and French armies abutted, turn left along the D197 for three kilometres until you reach the cross roads where Bernafay Wood faces you to the front right side. Turn right here along the D64 and after passing Bernafay Wood you will pass Trones Wood on your left before continuing into Guillemont.

A second route starts along the D938 Albert to Peronne road but then takes you through Fricourt and along the D64 past Mametz, Dantzig Alley Cemetery and the village of Montauban before arriving at the cross roads just south-west of Bernafay Wood. This route takes you through territory attacked by three divisions on the morning of 1st July, the 7th Division at Fricourt and Mametz, the 18th Division towards Pommiers Redoubt and the 30th Division towards Montauban, which all achieved some considerable degree of success in their attacks. When you arrive at the cross roads south-west of Bernafay Wood go straight ahead along the D64, past Trones Wood, towards Guillemont.

A third possibility lies along the D929 Albert to Bapaume road. Turn right into La Boisselle and continue along the D20 through

Contalmaison, Bazentin-le-Grand, Longueval and thence into Guillemont. This route takes you through much of the territory captured during the hot summer weeks of July 1916, and especially noteworthy here is the area east of Mametz Wood towards Trones Wood where the extraordinary Dawn Attack took place on 14th July.

Alternatively, Guillemont can be reached very simply from the Bapaume area. Take the D929 in the direction of Albert. Soon after leaving Bapaume take the road signed for Thilloy and Flers on your left. Follow this road, which soon joins the D10, into Flers and thence along the D197 into Longueval and then Guillemont. If you intend to study in the Guillemont-Ginchy-Combles area for any length of time then an alternativecentre to Albert is the small town of Rancourt, east of Combles on the D20 past the A1 motorway, where hotel accommodation is available.

There are no hotels within the area covered by this guide and the first thing you might therefore need to arrange is accommodation and tomorrow morning's breakfast. I have therefore identified below some of the available hotels and a number of "English" B&B houses where you can base yourself during a visit. However, for those of you with a tent or caravan and a more adventurous disposition, the Bellevue campsite in Authuille is a fine and central point on the Somme battlefield which can be reached from Guillemont via La Boisselle in twenty minutes by car. If you wish to avoid travelling back through Albert, take the D20 Longueval, Contalmaison to La Boisselle route thence across the D929 and take the road to Aveluy which is adjacent to La Boisselle's communal cemetery. From Aveluy follow the D151 into Authuille. The campsite is quiet and often frequented by people who share an interest in the Great War. The owner, Monsieur Desailly, and his family are always welcoming. The Bellevue campsite has been expanded to include a simple restaurant, reached thirty yards to the right as you look towards the main campsite entrance, where the food is both substantial and economical. Here you are within two minute's walk of the Authuille Military Cemetery and not far from the Auberge de la Vallee d'Ancre on the banks of the River Ancre. For many years this bar and restaurant has served decent food and drinks for as long as you cared to stay! The Auberge has been taken into new ownership in 1995 by Denis Bourgoyne who has already established a fine reputation for the quality of his food amongst the local community. There is another campsite at the village of Treux in the Ancre valley south west of Albert. This alternative is pleasantly shaded from the summer's heat but is too distant from the Guillemont area.

However, it can be bitterly cold camping in February! Therefore, for those of you who are travelling in style or during these colder and wetter months of the year, a roof over your heads may be welcome. The list identified below may be of some help, but it should not be inferred that the order is one of descending merit! To call for reservations from the UK dial 00 33, followed by the 9 digit number. In all these hotels, with one exception in Picquigny, you will find at least one person on the hotel's staff who can speak English.

Hotels:

The Royal Picardie ***, Route d'Amiens, 80300 Albert. Tel 322 75 37 00.

The Hotel de la Basilique **, 3 - 5 Rue Gambetta, 80300 Albert. Tel 322 75 04 71.

The Relais Fleuri **, 56 Avenue Faidherbe, 80300 Albert. Tel 322 75 08 11.

The Grande Hotel de la Paix *, 43 Rue Victor Hugo, 80300 Albert. Tel 322 75 01 64.

Les Etangs du Levant *, Rue du 1er Septembre, 80340 Bray sur Somme. Tel 322 76 70 00.

Auberge de Picquigny **, 112 Rue du 60 R.I., 80310 Picquigny. Tel 322 51 20 53.

Hotel Le Prieure. 17 Route National, 80860 Rancourt. Tel 322 85 04 43. This hotel is particularly well sited for access to the Guillemont area being located just six kilometres east through the small town of Combles.

B&B accommodation:

Auchonvillers – Beaumont Hamel. Comfortable and well appointed accommodation for up to eight people. Attractive grounds and interesting walks nearby. Evening meals and continental breakfast. Twenty minutes from Guillemont driving past Newfoundland Park, Thiepval and Pozieres. *Mike and Julie Renshaw.* Les Galets. Route de Beaumont, Auchonvillers. Tel: 322 76 28 79.

Auchonvillers. Five good rooms with en suite facilities and an interesting history, the centrepiece of which is the cellar still carved with the names of many soldiers who passed through in 1916. Bed, breakfast and evening meals by arrangement as well as a Tea Room for non residents. Again, access to Guillemont best undertaken by car. *Avril Williams.* 10 Rue Delattre, 80560 Auchonvillers. Tel: 322 76 23 66.

Courcelette. A distinctive farmhouse, self catering or meals provided. Situated right at the heart of the Somme Battlefields. This fine location provides the most straight forward access to Guillemont, less than ten minutes in a car. ***Paul Reed*** and ***Kieron Murphy***. Sommecourt, 39 Grande Rue, 80300 Courcelette. Tel: 322 74 01 35.

Martinpuich. A welcoming and comfortable house which can cater for up to eight people. This newly renovated house is situated at the heart of the 1916 Somme battlefield providing excellent and speedy access to Guillemont. Evening meals by request and continental breakfast. ***Colin*** and ***Lisa Gillard***. 54 Grand Rue, Martinpuich, 62450 Bapaume. Tel. 321 50 18 87.

The Guillemont Area

Once you are established it is time to see the surrounding locality and I suggest that, soon after you arrive, you would enjoy following the general tour explained in Chapter seven. However, in this first chapter I have attempted to give some definition to the boundaries of this guidebook and give a brief commentary to illustrate the importance of the area's history.

The boundaries to this guidebook run north from Maricourt, along the D197 until the cross-roads are reached, facing Bernafay Wood. The boundary then runs around the west and north of Bernafay Wood and north of Trones Wood to include the site of Waterlot Farm, north east

Guillemont village centre before the Great War. [Reed]

Reconstruction within Guillemont begins, soon after the Great War. [Reed]

of Guillemont. From there the boundary runs across the north of Guillemont and thence southwards past the east of the village along the course of the D20E towards Maurepas.

For some distance to the south of Guillemont the terrain rolls gently along a series of knolls or spurs, past Hardecourt valley and the Bois Faviere and Bois d'en Haut in the direction of the great Somme River. The most noticeable of these knolls stands south-west of Guillemont above and to the north of the Bois Faviere and Hardecourt-aux-Bois. At the northern end of this knoll in 1916 Maltz Horn Farm formed an important defensive position for the Germans, south-east of Trones

Guillemont village centre, present day.

TRONES WOOD   BERNAFAY WOOD   MONTAUBAN

GUILLEMONT CEMETERY

SITE OF STATION

GUILLEMONT VILLAGE

The battle arena of the summer of 1916. The Germans were pushed back from the woods to the village of Guillemont from where they were dislodged in September. [Cave]

Wood. But only when you arrive on the D938 Albert to Peronne road is it possible to appreciate just what a significant course the River Somme cuts across this area of France. South of the D938 the land falls away sharply and you can look down on the Somme as it meanders idly, a great basin of water meadows, lakes, pools and canalised waterways which make a considerable natural barrier. The Bois Faviere objective was captured by the French on the morning of 1st July 1916, along with the village of Curlu which lies adjacent to one of the huge sweeping meanders which characterise the Somme's sedate progress in this area.

Five kilometres north of the River Somme the chalk upland terrain around Bernafay Wood, Trones Wood, Longueval and Guillemont is on first glance seemingly devoid of significant geographical features. Over such porous base rock the fields are without streams. During the fighting for Guillemont and Falfemont Farm the lack of water posed ever present difficulties for the men and their transport and supply units. Here there are no sudden and impressive slopes such as those which provided such easily defensible positions to the German army on 1st July 1916 at the villages of Thiepval or Ovillers. From Guillemont a shallow valley, Caterpillar Valley, runs westwards, through Trones Wood, north of Bernafay Wood, thence past Caterpillar Wood, south of Mametz Wood and then south-westwards towards Fricourt where it occasionally produces a trickle of water known as the Willow Stream. In the Trones Wood-Guillemont area what higher

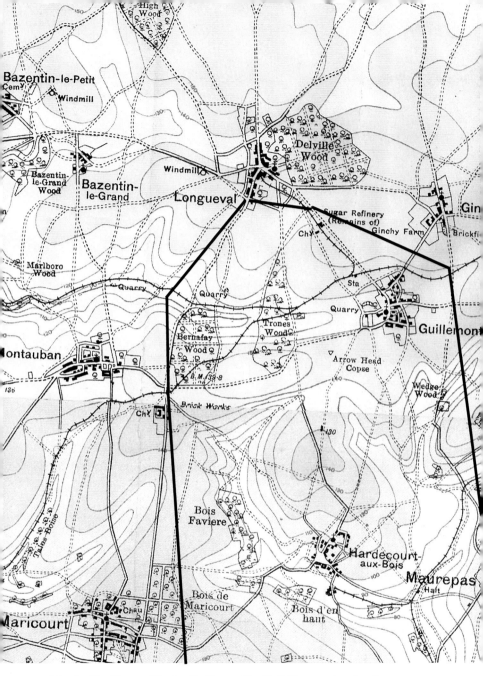

Map 1. The Trones Wood – Guillemont battlefield area, showing the pre-war geography of the area. This is taken from the 1:40,000 sheets which accompanied the Official History volume detailing the fighting leading to the first day of the Battle of the Somme.

25

ground is of discernible significance lies to the north, around Longueval and Delville Wood, where the highest elevations are a little over 150 metres above sea level. The advantage in height enjoyed by the German army at Delville Wood ensured that the capture of Trones Wood would be carried out amidst the most terrible ordeal of shellfire since the wood and its approaches were observed from that higher ground to the north. As the Official History put the situation so succinctly:

> 'Facing Longueval, in the German 2nd Position, Trones Wood stretches down the southern slope of Caterpillar Valley as far as the foot of its northern slope; east of the wood the valley extends as a shallow trough to Guillemont, which was also in the 2nd Position. Thus the wood was commanded at close range both from the north and the east, and there was little chance of holding it whilst the enemy sat in Longueval and Guillemont. Captured it might be, at a price, but only by permission of the Germans could it be held.'[3]

Running north-west from Guillemont, past Longueval and Pozieres, the higher ground persists all the way to Thiepval in a great spine of elevated ground which overlooked the British positions at the outset of the Battle of the Somme. At Thiepval that elevated ridge falls away steeply into valley of the River Ancre and it was this height which the British army sought so desperately to attain during the long and bitter months of the Somme campaign.

1. I shall subsequently usually refer to Hardecourt-aux-Bois simply as Hardecourt throughout this guide.
2. Bois des Troncs on your IGN maps of the area, and also on pre-war French maps of the area.
3. *Military Operations. France and Belgium. 1916.* Vol 2. pp37.

Second Lieutenant Jack Fearnhead, 1/7th King's (Liverpool), 55th (Territorial) Division, from whose diary a brief extract appears opposite. He had enlisted, in September 1914, as a private.

Chapter Two

THE EVENTS WHICH BROUGHT THE BRITISH ARMY TO TRONES WOOD[1]

Men had assembled for months before the 1916 Somme battles commenced. Many had, at the time they were sucked into its seemingly inexhaustibly grim appetite, little idea of what terribleness they would face. Thousands of British soldiers thought the event would presage the end of war. Some, like Jack Fearnhead, were well aware their departure from home, and all they held dear, was a step into the unknown. As he left Southampton in the late evening of 26 May 1916, this young subaltern with the 1/7th King's, 55th (Territorial) Division, recorded that:

> *'At 10p.m. the anchors were drawn up, and steam put on, and shortly we left behind the last solid view of Southampton, a vista of trees on each flank, broken on the right by the towers and chimneys of Osborne, and dead astern by the chimneys and roofs and occasional masts of Southampton, all silhouetted fiercely against one of the most perfect sunsets man ever saw. The sea astern a marvellous electric blue, no waves, a few very small wavelets not sufficient to break the blue in the smallest degree. The sky above it an artist's palette of colour, brilliant flaming red immediately above the horizon, shading off gently through all the colours known, and some for which we have no words, through yellows, greens, blues, to a deep unknown purple overhead. It was truly wonderful, and the whole effect inspired one with an intense desire for something indefinite, something intangible, perhaps for further knowledge of the Creator of so wonderful a scene – of God.'[2]*

It was perhaps the last moment of beauty that these men would ever witness.

On the morning of 1 July 1916 the British army, in conjunction with the French, launched a massive assault along a frontage running continuously from their positions facing Serre all the way south to those facing Montauban. South of Montauban the British and French armies joined at the village of Maricourt and the impact which the French artillery made during their part of those initial bombardment was immensely helpful to the British. East and to the south of Maricourt the French attack was due to continue past the River Somme.

27

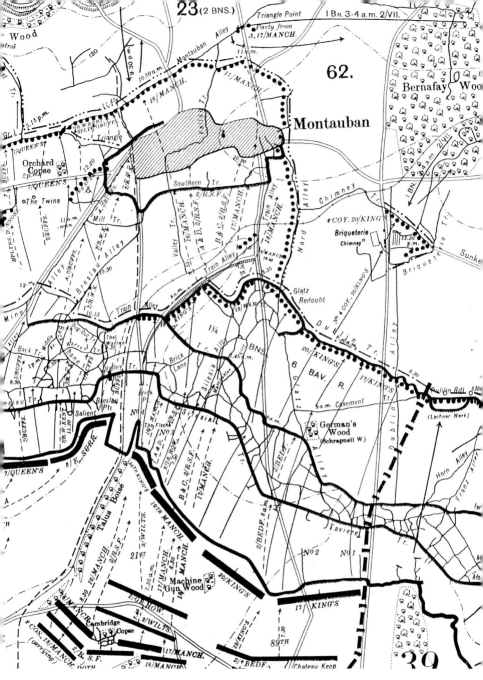

Map 2. The dispositions of XIII Corps' men in the vicinity of Maricourt /
Montauban before and after their successful attack on 1st July 1916.
Taken from the *Official History* series of maps, 1916 Vol I.

The British unit whose attack was developed from the Maricourt sector was the 30th Division. Their objective was the capture of Montauban. To effect this advance the 30th Division employed the Liverpool Pals to make the initial advance across the German front line positions facing Maricourt whilst the Manchester Pals would secure Montauban village itself in the final stages of the attack. Montauban was one of many strongly fortified Intermediate Positions in this area between the Germans' front lines and their main Second Position. On the right of the British 30th Division stood the French army's 39th Division whose first day objective was the capture of Bois Favier. The 30th Division included among its ranks four of the Manchester Pals battalions and four of the Liverpool Pals[3].

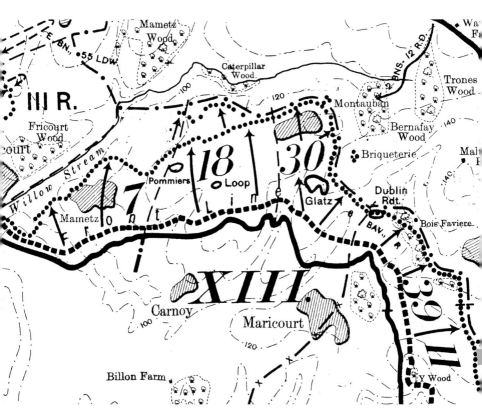

Map 3. The Objectives allotted to the 7th, 18th and 30th British Divisions along with the French 39th and 11th Divisions for the 1st July, taken from the *Official History* series of maps, 1916 Vol I.

The attacks made by the 30th Division, and that by the 18th and 7th Divisions to their left, were, by contrast with much that occurred elsewhere this day, hugely successful. All along the southern arm of the British army's frontage, from Fricourt to Montauban, a very substantial advance was made which reflects enormously well upon the resilience and determination of the soldiers in this part of the battlefront. Elsewhere, with the possible exception of the Ulstermen at Schwaben Redoubt north of Thiepval, the story was one of unremitting disaster. The advance from Fricourt - Mametz along to Montauban was the only one of substance which was consolidated and held by the end of that day. Just north of Montauban the Manchester Pals had captured Montauban Alley whilst the Liverpool Pals held the Briqueterie, southeast of Montauban and south of Bernafay Wood.

As a consequence this southern sector of the British frontage, adjacent to those advances made by the French, would now become the focus of the British army's attempts to wring some advantage out of their tragedy on 1 July.

Perhaps one of the most inexplicable issues which has since been debated at great length is why Rawlinson failed to capitalise on the success at Montauban on 1 July. Here the Manchester Pals had repelled German counter attacks in the area around Triangle Point between 3 and 4 am on the morning of 2nd July and the village was secure. It seemed that most of the German infantry reserves had been committed and that his artillery was in a state of disarray. One problem was that by the morning of 2 July the Maricourt area south of Montauban was very congested with troop movements, both British and French. The French Sixth Army had issued orders at 8.30 am on the morning of 1 July pointing out that the attack of their XX Corps on the German second positions including Hardecourt would depend upon the British attacking Bernafay and Trones Woods. At 10.30 am on the 2nd a further French Sixth Army order simply instructed their men on these locations to stand fast.

During the morning of 2 July the 30th Division's field howitzers shelled Bernafay Wood with thermite shells in an attempt to set the woodland on fire. Later in the day the wood was scoured by patrols who captured a number of prisoners. This was the day that Haig had arrived early at Fourth Army HQ urging that the success at Montauban should be exploited and that attacks should be made along the whole southern arm of the battlefield, taking the lines of German trenches facing westwards, to the north of Fricourt, in the rear. However those attacks were not forthcoming as Rawlinson concentrated his efforts

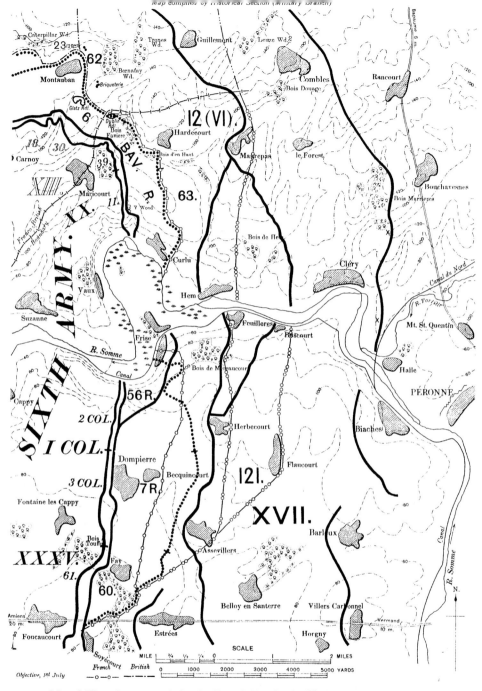

Map 4. The advance made by the French XX Corps (Sixth Army) between
Bois Faviere and Curlu on the morning of 1st July 1916. *Official History,
1916* Vol 1.

Longueval Church   B o i s   F   a

B o i s

Panorama of the front taken in the summer of 1916 close to where the British and French lines abutted.

throughout the day on frontal attacks being made in the Thiepval – Ovillers – La Boisselle areas. By 3 July the divisions within XIII Corps were still occupied with consolidation yet patrols in Bernafay Wood were still able to report that it was undefended. It was only at 3.15 pm that Congreve, XIII Corps' commanding officer, ordered the 30th Division to occupy the wood. That attack was undertaken at 9.00 pm by soldiers of 27 Brigade[4] operating under control of the 30th Division

Bernafay Wood today, photographed from its southern aspect.

es Trones

Waterlot Chimney

ere

and was achieved with the loss of only six casualties! In terms of the subsequent history of attempts to capture woodlands on the Somme battlefield this was an extraordinary lapse on the part of the Germans.

At this stage it was also clear that Trones Wood was held more strongly. However Rawlinson was still strangely reluctant to give emphasis to his troops success in the south, believing that the capture of Bernafay Wood had created an awkward re-entrant at the junction of the British and French armies. Nevertheless, it was decided at the Corps commanders conference, held that afternoon of 3 July, that every preparation should be made for an attack on the German second position in the Longueval to Bazentin-le-Petit area.

It was therefore self-evident that Trones Wood would have to be captured before such an attack could take place.

4th - 8th July in the Bernafay – Trones Wood area

On 4 July it was abundantly clear that the German defences north of La Boisselle were still secure. By contrast, in the area between the Albert – Bapaume road in the north and the Amiens – Vermand road south of the River Somme the German position was relatively weak. In view of what had been happening at Verdun the German army had been surprised by the effectiveness of the French whose advance south of

DELVILLE WOOD

CATERPILLAR VALLEY

TRONES WOOD

The view towards Trones Wood from the south-east corner of Bernafay Wood.

the river had seen the capture of many German troops and artillery units. Here the French Sixth Army had already advanced some three miles towards Biaches and Barleux. However, this day, 4 July, the weather began to play havoc with the British attempts to press forward towards the German second positions. Showers turned to a

The view towards Maltz Horn Farm and the Hardecourt area from the sunken lane south of Bernafay Wood.

MALTZ HORN FARM

HARDECOURT

SUNKEN LANE

thunderstorm in the afternoon and the British trenches and supply routes became a quagmire. During these three difficult days, between 4th to the 6th inclusive, both the British and French gave emphasis to preparing for their attack, due on 7th, against the Hardecourt - Trones Wood - Mametz Wood and Contalmaison positions. Although south of the Somme things had gone well, to the north of the Somme the French were clamped in the same difficulties which beset the British. The fulcrum around which this issue swung at the junction of the British and French armies was the problem of capturing the Trones woodland area.

As we have seen, the combined French – British Hardecourt – Trones Wood attack was due on the 7th. However, on 6 July German counter attacks at Bois Faviere, which succeeded in re-capturing the northern edge of that wood, ensured that the attack on Hardecourt and Trones Wood was postponed until the 8th. Overnight, 7/8th July, the weather was wet and the underfoot conditions continued to hamper the British and French troops preparing to make this attack. The British would employ the 30th Division, commanded by Major-General Shea, a unit which had already been in the area for months and whose men had performed so brilliantly on the morning of 1 July to effect the capture of Montauban.

The plan to capture Trones Wood

The Allied attack would be in two stages. The first stage, timed for 8.00 am, would be undertaken jointly, in part by the French who were due to capture Maltz Horn Trench, in front of Maltz Horn knoll between Hardecourt and the junction between the two armies, whilst the British captured the continuation of the Maltz Horn Trench north towards Trones Wood and the southern half of the wood itself. Later, at a time to be agreed upon by the local commanders, the French would attack Hardecourt and the Maltz Horn knoll to its north whilst the British would attack Maltz Horn Farm's rubble and capture the remainder of Trones Wood.

The British faced a severe problem in that the distance from the Briqueterie to the German held Maltz Horn Trench was across 1,100 to 1,500 yards of open and fire-swept land. Further south the French faced a much narrower prospect. Congreve therefore decided to capture the southern part of Trones as a preliminary operation. Trones Wood was effectively divided by the course of two light railway lines which passed through the woodland. The more significant line was the Albert to Peronne light railway which passed between Montauban and the Briqueterie, thence through Bernafay Wood, where there was a station in its south-western corner, and Trones Wood before passing Guillemont on the north side of that village. The other line, effectively a branch of the main line, approached from the confines of Caterpillar Valley just north of Bernafay and joined the Albert - Peronne line just east of Trones Wood. Congreve's plan had the advantage that the approach to Trones Wood from the southern end of Bernafay Wood was not observed from Longueval. Once the southern end of Trones was secured the British attack towards Maltz Horn Trench and Farm could be made in a south-easterly direction across the shallow head of Maltz Horn valley, which was hidden from the German Second Position.

1. Whether by accident or design the military cartographers who mapped this area for the British Army in the years both before and during the Great War often changed the spelling of locations. Trones Wood is a corruption of Bois des Troncs.

2. Extract from Jack Fearnhead's Diary, May 26th, 1916.

3. The 30th Division consisted of:
    21 Brigade.
        18th Kings (Liverpool Pals).
        2nd Green Howards.
        2nd Wiltshire.
        19th Manchester (Pals).
    89 Brigade.
        17th Kings (Liverpool Pals).
        19th Kings (Liverpool Pals).
        20th Kings (Liverpool Pals).
        2nd Bedfordshire.
    90 Brigade.
        2nd Royal Scots Fusiliers.
        16th Manchester (Pals).
        17th Manchester (Pals).
        18th Manchester (Pals).
    Divisional Pioneers: 11th South Lancashire.

4. 27 Brigade were part of the 9th (Scottish) Division. The two battalions which captured Bernafay Wood at so little cost were the 6th KOSBs and the 12th Royal Scots.

Chapter Three

THE BATTLE FOR CONTROL OF TRONES WOOD

The events of 8th July

At 8 am on the morning of 8th July the British attempt to capture Trones Wood began. It was to prove a long and arduous process. For some hours prior to the infantry assault the Corps' heavy artillery and the field guns of both the 18th and 30th Divisions had fired with relatively little impact on the German positions. On the right the French artillery barrage was far more effective, reducing the III/123rd Reserve Regiment to just two officers and 150 others. The initial British attack on Trones Wood was undertaken by the 2nd Green Howards of 21 Brigade. The men moved forward through Bernafay Wood struggling with the dense undergrowth and smashed trees which only served to worsen the trauma of artillery shells which were already falling around them. Leaving the confines of the wood the Green Howards began to cross the open ground towards Trones Wood, breasting the slight rise which initially shielded them from view.

As soon as the men came into view of the Germans in Trones Wood, the Green Howards' men were caught in a curtain of fire from machine guns and two field guns firing over open sights from the edge of the woodland. There were heavy casualties and the Green Howards were withdrawn, the 2nd Wiltshire being ordered to renew the attack at 10.30 am. In view of what had happened, Brigadier General Sackville-West arranged a postponement until 1.00 pm. Already the plan of a combined Anglo-French operations in the Trones – Hardecourt area was breaking down and a melange of local initiatives and Corps orders began to emerge as the norm within this area.

On the right of the British the French assault had gone ahead as

Major General Shea, the 30th Division's commanding officer.

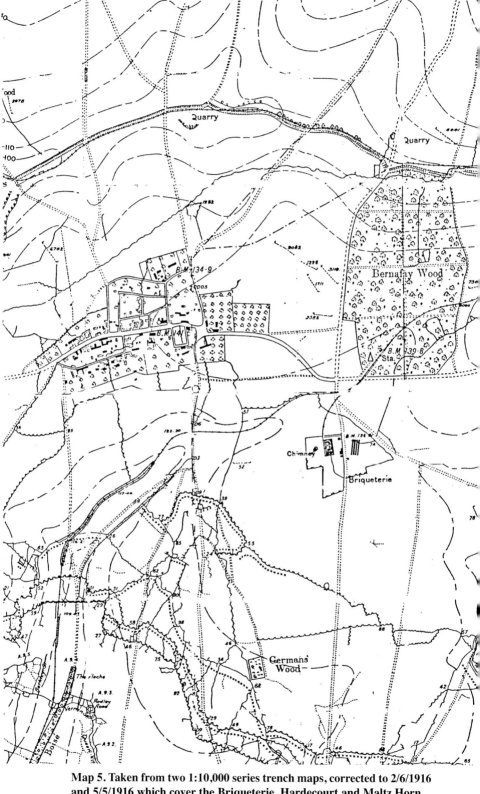

Map 5. Taken from two 1:10,000 series trench maps, corrected to 2/6/1916 and 5/5/1916 which cover the Briqueterie, Hardecourt and Maltz Horn

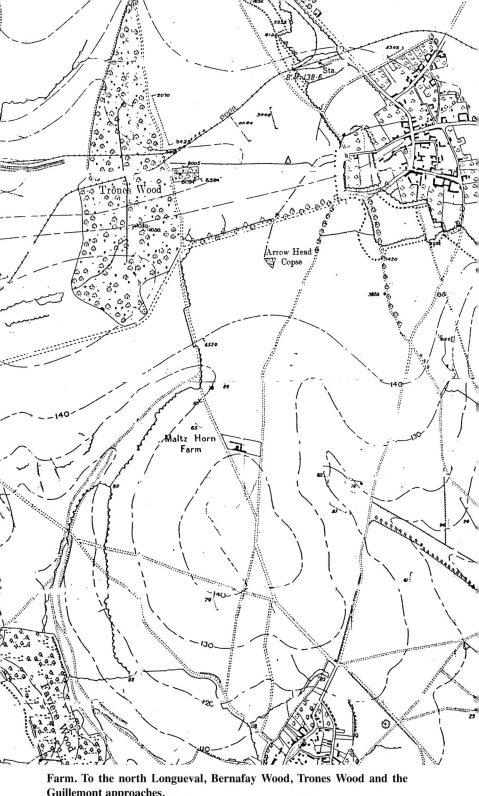

Farm. To the north Longueval, Bernafay Wood, Trones Wood and the Guillemont approaches.

planned at 10.05 am, capturing their sector of Maltz Horn Trench up to a position opposite the site of Maltz Horn Farm. Because of the failure of 21 Brigade's men to get into Trones Wood the Frenchmen's left flank was completely exposed to machine gun fire from that wood. As a consequence, at 12.20 pm, Congreve ordered that Shea's 30th Division, in order to cover the French left, attack towards Maltz Horn Farm and Trones Wood from the direction of the Briqueterie, as the Official History put it, 'even if he had to employ his whole division.'!

Fortunately this process had already got off to a good start on the initiative of the 2nd Wiltshires, one company of which had worked their way up to the head of Maltz Horn Valley[1] along the sunken lane leading south-east from the Briqueterie. These men had then taken a part of Maltz Horn Trench allotted to the British part of the attack, and they had been later reinforced by a company of the 19th Manchesters (4th Pals) who linked up with the French on their right. Maltz Horn Farm was now little more than a barely perceptible heap of rubble between the two lines facing each other across the knoll, the Germans having withdrawn to the eastern slopes of the knoll. However, there was still a gap between the two companies of the Wiltshires and Manchesters adjacent to the French facing Maltz Horn Farm and the southern end of Trones Wood.

Throughout the rest of the afternoon of 8th July a number of further British battalions were drawn into the attempts to capture Trones Wood. The first men to get into the wood reached that objective as a result of an attack at about 1.00 pm by the remaining three companies of the 2nd Wiltshires from Bernafay Wood. Although, like the 2nd Green Howards before them, the Wiltshires suffered heavy casualties, small groups of men reached the south-eastern edge of Trones Wood where they entrenched themselves and began to construct a further trench to their right, facing north, to protect their flank. Two further companies of the 18th King's and one of the 19th Manchesters managed to get up to help with this process of consolidation and by nightfall the 18th Manchesters of 90 Brigade had arrived to prepare for an attempt, due the following morning, to renew the attack on Trones Wood.

The events of 9th July

By now it was clear that what had been described as preliminary operations, designed to ensure the success of the general attack on the German second position due soon[2], were taking on a severity and momentum of their own. The Official History comments that:

40

'It so happened that in these preliminary operations several days of hard and costly fighting did not achieve complete success; yet, if the three localities [Contalmaison, Mametz Wood and Trones Wood] had been included in the general attack against the German 2nd Position, they might, if stoutly defended, have disorganised the assault and destroyed its impetus before the main objectives were approached. Certain it is that some penalty had to be paid for the failure to take advantage of the opportunities which had offered themselves on this front immediately after the first day of the offensive.'[3]

The cost of that tardiness would be born, in large part, by the Manchester and Liverpool Pals units of the 30th Division.

The first events of this day were marked, at 3.00 am, by a successful advance by the men of 2nd Royal Scots of 90 Brigade who again made use of the sunken lane leading south-eastwards from the Briqueterie. By this route the 2nd Royal Scots gained the centre of Maltz Horn Trench, rushing the ruins of the farm and then bombing their way northwards up Maltz Horn Trench in the direction of Trones Wood. By 7.00 am the Royal Scots had reached the Guillemont road which ran towards that village from the south-eastern corner of the wood.

Looking towards Guillemont from the south-eastern corner of Trones Wood.

The second, and seemingly decisive event, was the attack made by the 17th Manchesters on Trones Wood. This attack was timed at 3.00 am from Bernafay Wood. The men were greatly hampered by gas shells and the misting of their eye pieces in the damp drizzle laden atmosphere. Consequently their advance across the ground between the two woods only took place some three hours after it should have occurred! Nevertheless, the men passed successfully through Trones Wood, reaching its eastern border at approximately 8.00 am. There the 17th Manchesters joined with the 2nd Royal Scots and then pushed patrols into the northern end of the wood.

Trones Wood was now, early on the morning of 9th July, in British hands.

The situation was soon to change. Within hours, soon after mid-day, the Germans had organised a systematic shelling of Trones Wood and its western approaches. The 17th Manchesters suffered particularly severely on the eastern limits of the wood and in view of what seemed an imminent counter attack the men were ordered at 3.00 pm to withdraw. They began to fall back towards Bernafay Wood. Unfortunately one detachment, which the order failed to reach, was left within the wood's confines. At 3.30 pm the Germans began to develop a general counter attack from the Maltz Horn Farm area all the way to the northern limits of Trones Wood. In view of the 17th Manchesters' retirement the 18th Manchesters were also forced to pull back, in their case towards the Briqueterie, leaving one company in the south-eastern corner of Trones Wood. Bearing in mind what was happening to their north the 2nd Royal Scots then withdrew from Maltz Horn Trench joining with the company of the 18th Manchesters just inside the south-eastern corner of Trones, leaving a block just clear of the wood. Although the Royal Scots and 18th Manchesters drove off the Germans facing them the Germans succeeded in penetrating the bulk of the northern end of the wood north of the Guillemont road. As the Germans pressed through the wood the isolated detachment of 17th Manchesters was overwhelmed after stout resistance.

Thus, by 4.00 pm on 9 July the greater part of Trones Wood was back in German hands. The German's artillery, arrayed in a great sweep from Maurepas, east of Hardecourt, to Bazentin-le-Grand, completely dominated the area and it seemed likely that any subsequent British counter attacks designed to recapture Trones would be costly.

Initially that counter attack was the responsibility of the 16th Manchesters, the 1st Manchester Pals. Their attack was launched from

A German observation post in Trones Wood.

the sunken lane, which ran from the Briqueterie towards Hardecourt, at 6.40 pm. Their objective was to re-secure the southern portion of the wood and cover the left of the Royal Scots who should have been in possession of Maltz Horn Trench. The 16th Manchester's attack succeeded in advancing to support the Royal Scots well but was unable to secure the southern part of the wood. As a consequence the 16th Manchesters dug in about 60 yards south of Trones where they spent an uncomfortable and exposed night.

The events of 10th July

During the early hours of the night of 9/10th the 16th Manchesters sent patrols out into Trones Wood to attempt a clarification of the situation there. Progress in the pitch black amongst the devastation was tortuously slow. It was decided to make an advance soon after first light at which time a preliminary bombardment was fired on the wood. At 4.00 am the 16th Manchesters, to whom a company of the 4th South African Regiment had been attached[4], began to advance in sections northwards through the wood. The advance proved almost impossible to co-ordinate and many men became disorientated. However, some determined groups passed along the whole length of the wood and returned to report it clear of German soldiers. Those reports were mistaken since some Germans had not evacuated the wood when the preliminary bombardment had struck. Soon, on the western side of the wood, fighting broke out within the confines of Longueval Alley, a trench which led from the northern end of Trones across the upper reaches of Caterpillar Valley into the north-eastern tip of Bernafay Wood. The focus of this fighting moved to Central Trench at the northern tip of the wood. Whilst this struggle continued a large number of Germans advanced from the Waterlot Farm area, capturing several of the 16th Manchesters' sections and re-occupying the western side of the wood.

By 8.00 am on the morning of 10th July only the south-eastern part of Trones Wood remained in British hands again. Corpses littered the smoking woodland's wreckage and the smell of putrefaction hung heavily in the air. The men unfortunate enough to be within Trones Wood were plagued with flies and the awful sights and stench of corruption. Concern was mounting that failure to capture Trones Wood might compromise the chances of success of the imminent attack on the German main Second Position east of Longueval. However, the remainder of the day was quiet and the 30th Division took the opportunity to relieve 90 Brigade by 89 Brigade under the cover of darkness.

The events of 11th – 12th July

On the morning of 11th July the decision was made by the British that Trones Wood should be flattened by an overwhelmingly heavy artillery barrage. Accordingly the south eastern portion of the wood was evacuated and the 2nd Royal Scots replaced by the 20th King's in Maltz Horn Trench. The plan was that, as soon as the bombardment ended the 20th King's would bomb their way northwards into the south-eastern corner of Trones Wood. The 2nd Bedfordshires were arrayed in the sunken lane south-east of the Briqueterie and they would advance into the southern part of the wood linking with the King's who would join on the Bedfords' right flank. At 2.40 am XIII Corps' heavy guns, as well as all the available divisional guns in the area, opened an intensive bombardment of Trones Wood.

Three quarters of an hour after the bombardment began the 20th King's began their attempt to bomb northwards along Maltz Horn Trench. Initially all went well, many German soldiers were killed and two machine guns captured. Unfortunately the 20th King's did not

Tangled undergrowth, shattered tree stumps and branches of Trones Wood made it difficult for troops of both sides in the fierce fighting for its possession.

reach their objective, stopping a little short of the strong-point[5] on the eastern side of Trones where the Guillemont road lay. The 2nd Bedfords' advance was also inconclusive. They advanced against heavy machine-gun fire which drove their two right hand companies too far to the right. The two left companies did make the western side of Trones between Trones Alley and the Albert – Peronne light railway line. These men tried to work northwards and eastwards but found the Germans resolute in defence behind an impenetrable tangle of utterly shattered timber, undergrowth, torn tree roots and entangled barbed wire. Meanwhile the two right companies of the 2nd Bedfords worked their way from the upper reaches of Maltz Horn valley into the south eastern side of Trones Wood, but were unable to progress past the German held strong-point on the Guillemont road.

Throughout the rest of the morning fighting continued within the wood and to the south in the confines of Maltz Horn Trench. By midday the Germans, who had been reinforced, cleared the northern end of Trones, forcing one company of the Bedfords back into Bernafay Wood. Fortunately the British were able to fend off further German counter attacks planned for later that evening. Information

A carrying party of British troops move forward with supplies of ammunition and grenades, from Bernafay Wood, during July 1916.

about this planned attack was found on a German officer captured by the French in the afternoon and, as a consequence, a constant defensive artillery barrage was maintained between Guillemont and Trones Wood as well as east of Guillemont with the intention of breaking up the assembly of German units in those vicinities.

That evening the 17th King's attacked the southern end of the wood from the confines of the sunken lane, south-east of the Briqueterie. These Liverpool Pals successfully took control of the southern end of the wood from German soldiers of the 182nd Regiment, re-wiring and re-digging their trenches along the south-eastern side of the wood.

The following morning, 12 July, the process of consolidation went ahead with the utmost urgency. With the help of the divisional engineers a new trench was begun to link the 17th King's with the Bedfordshire's positions. The process was made almost impossible by the depth of shattered timber, torn undergrowth and wire. Nevertheless, this new trench took shape, running intermittently south-westwards across the wood from the Guillemont Road junction in the east, dividing the small British controlled southern end of the wood from the north which was still in German hands. Whilst this digging was in process German counter attacks against Maltz Horn Trench and Trones Wood were launched at 8.30 pm but were effectively driven off by the prompt use of artillery. During the hours of darkness overnight on 12/13th the trench was further improved but at best the situation was described by incoming troops as 'only a shallow trench with a low parapet held in patches.'

This panorama shows both Bernafay (left) and Trones Woods. German shells are bursting in the vicinity of Bernafay, to the centre-left of the photograph. At this time German troops were occupying Trones Wood.

It was at this stage that the 30th Division was finally withdrawn from the Trones Wood area. The Division had been engaged in the Maricourt – Montauban sector all year. They had effected the successful capture of Montauban and the Briqueterie on 1 July and had fought desperately for control of Trones Wood. In the five days fighting between 8 and 12 July the division had lost over 2,300 casualties amongst all ranks. They were replaced by Major General Ivor Maxse's 18th Division, which fought on the 30th Division's left on 1 July and had suffered 3,300 casualties that day.

13th and 14th July – desperate measures to capture Trones Wood

It was now agreed between Rawlinson and Haig that the attack on the German main Second Position between Longueval and Bazentin-le-Petit would take place on 14th July at first light, 3.20 am. The plan for this attack was necessarily complex, the troops' assembly would have to take place at night. Men drawn from four divisions would participate and it was imperative that the minimum of disruption which might corrupt the chances of this bold initiative's success should occur. It was thus essential that Trones Wood be captured as soon as was humanly possible.

It was now the turn of 55 Brigade, 18th Division, to take their place in the ebb and flow of events at Trones Wood and Maltz Horn Trench.[6] Two further battalions, the 12th Middlesex and the 6th Northamptons, were attached to 55 Brigade as support units. They would be vital in the following three days fighting. Having taken over these positions, before dawn on the 13th, 55 Brigade was ordered to make a new attempt on the northern end of the wood at 7.00 pm, after a two hour bombardment by the 30th Division's artillery. The barrage was

concentrated upon Central Trench and the area facing Longueval Alley. At 7.00 pm the 7th Buffs began their advance along Maltz Horn Trench but again, as with the 20th King's before them, failed to reach the strong-point on the eastern side of wood astride the Guillemont road. Meanwhile the 7th Royal West Kent attacked from the new trench running across the wood. In the chaos of tumbled timber and the onset of darkness the attack quickly lost any sense of unified direction. From their north, German survivors in Central Trench opened fire at very short range. Some 150 of the West Kents found their way to the eastern side of the wood, just south of the strong-point, and imagined that they had succeeded in reaching the northern apex of the wood and that the wood was therefore in British hands! Throughout the night isolated groups of the West Kents found themselves fighting for control of small patches of woodland, out of contact with their comrades or the Brigade HQ. On the north-west of Trones Wood an attack made from Longueval Alley by the 7th Queens was repulsed by a combination of rifle, machine-gun and artillery fire, the last being co-ordinated from the higher ground which the Germans still enjoyed along the Longueval to Bazentin-le-Petit ridge. One small group of bombers from the 7th Queens commanded by Lieutenant B.C.Haggard did however manage to get into the northern tip of the wood, having fought their way up Longueval Alley, and here they stayed throughout the night.

It was not until after midnight that XIII Corps' commander, Lieutenant General Congreve, was told by Maxse, 18th Division's commanding officer, that 55 Brigade's attack on the northern end of Trones Wood had failed. The general attack on the German Second Position was now due in three hours, less than 300 yards away from Trones Wood. The men involved in that attack were already engaged in their extraordinary and silent assembly by night. As yet they had not been seen.

At 12.45 am, amidst the drizzle and dank mist of morning, 54 Brigade, commanded by Brigadier General Shoubridge, was told by Congreve that his brigade would have to capture Trones Wood. The success of the 9th Division's attack on Longueval was dependant upon that fact. Meanwhile, the German gunners 'continued to shell the wood heavily, not caring apparently if they killed their own men as well as ours.'

There was no time for reconnaissance. Shoubridge decided that only a simple plan would stand any chance of success. His men would sweep through from south to north, establishing a defensive flank on

MONTAUBAN

MALTZ HORN VALLEY

BERNAFAY WOOD

TRONES WOOD

HARDECOURT

The terrain due south of Trones Wood across which the 6th Northamptons advanced on the morning of 14th July. Photographed from close to Maltz Horn Farm Crucifix.

the right, the eastern perimeter of the wood, as they progressed. The 12th Middlesex would lead the way, the 6th Northamptonshires would follow up and establish the defensive flank. However, in the chaos of troop movements, around the sunken lane south-east of the Briqueterie, the Middlesex battalion were slow to get up and Lieutenant Colonel F.A.Maxwell of the Middlesex, in local charge of the operation, decided to put the Northamptons in the lead and use his own Middlesex men to make the flank guard as and when they could be assembled. In support of this operation the 7th Bedfords and the 11th Royal Fusiliers were moved up from Trigger Valley to positions in Dublin Trench and Maricourt village.

Advancing from the sunken lane at about 3.00 am the Northamptons covered the 1000 yards of open ground south of Trones Wood under a terrifying barrage of 5.9' shells, the survivors gaining the southern perimeter at 4.30 am. This was just minutes before the Dawn Attack on the German main Second Position was begun, less than three hundred yards to the west of Trones Wood. By 6.00 am the Northampton's men were in control of much of Central Trench. Greatly thinned in numbers the Northamptons nevertheless continued to advance northwards but became increasingly disorientated amidst the debris and ruination which surrounded them. Eventually the men halted at the small copse[7] which projects from the eastern side of the wood – believing this to be the northern apex of Trones. The men then

51

lined the eastern edge of the wood from the railway track down to the strong-point on the Guillemont road.

There now followed one of the most original and memorable events of the Great War. Its instigator was Lieutenant Colonel Frank A. Maxwell who had moved into the wood at 8.00 am with the bulk of his battalion, the 12th Middlesex.[8]

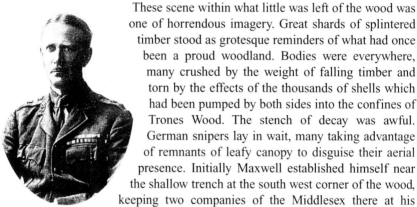

These scene within what little was left of the wood was one of horrendous imagery. Great shards of splintered timber stood as grotesque reminders of what had once been a proud woodland. Bodies were everywhere, many crushed by the weight of falling timber and torn by the effects of the thousands of shells which had been pumped by both sides into the confines of Trones Wood. The stench of decay was awful. German snipers lay in wait, many taking advantage of remnants of leafy canopy to disguise their aerial presence. Initially Maxwell established himself near the shallow trench at the south west corner of the wood, keeping two companies of the Middlesex there at his disposal. In front of him soldiers were crawling around trying to identify friend or foe, firing blindly. It was a hellish cauldron. Now, at 8.00 am, Maxwell went boldly forward to reconnoitre the situation himself. He found scattered groups of the 7th Royal West Kent's men around the south eastern corner. They had been there all night! Nearby were other groups of Middlesex and Northamptons who were exhausted and disorientated.

F.A.Maxwell, V.C., C.S.I., D.S.O., after his promotion to the rank of Brigadier.

Nevertheless, by dint of extraordinary powers of organisation and leadership Maxwell inspired these men to the final capture of Trones Wood.

One company of the Middlesex were detailed to attack and capture the strong-point on the Guillemont road. This they would do in conjunction with the 7th Buffs who were in Maltz Horn Trench. This manoeuvre was successful and completed by 9.00 am. Within the wood Maxwell sent an officer from the groups he had found in the south eastern corner across the wood on a compass bearing until he reached the western perimeter. Behind him a great crocodile of Maxwell's men were strung out across the wood. As the officer reached the perimeter the order was given to face right and the advance began, shoulder to shoulder. The wood was so devastated that any normal signs of direction were utterly missing. The men moved ahead, guided at every step by compass. To maintain the men's nerve in the face of constant sniping Maxwell ordered them to fire from the hip into the undergrowth and branches ahead of them. At the point where the Albert - Peronne light railway entered on the western side of the wood a machine-gun post was encountered and Maxwell, with perhaps 70 of his men, surrounded and captured the post, killing all its occupants. For a while no Germans were seen but more serious opposition was met at the second of the two light railway lines. In a letter, written to his wife, Maxwell gives an insight into this extraordinary story:

'I had meant only to organise and start the line, and then get back to my loathsome ditch, back near the edge of the wood, so as to be in communication by runners with the brigade and world outside. But... I immediately found that without my being there the thing would collapse in a few minutes. Sounds vain, perhaps, but there is nothing of vanity about it, really. So off I went with the line, leading it, pulling it on, keeping its direction, keeping it from its hopeless (and humanly natural) desire to get into a single file behind me, instead of a long line either side.

'Soon I made them advance with fixed bayonets, and ordered them, by way of encouraging themselves, to fire ahead of them into the tangle all the way. This was a good move, and gave them confidence... The Germans couldn't face a long line offering no scattered groups to be killed, and they began to bolt, first back, then, as the wood became narrow, they bolted out to the sides, and with rifle and automatic guns we slew them.

'Right up to the very top this went on, and I could have had a much bigger bag, except that I did not want to show my people out of the wood, or too much out, for fear of letting the German artillery know how we had progressed, and so enable them to plaster the wood parri passu *with our advance...'*[9]

During the final sweep towards the apex of the wood Sergeant William Ewart Boulter of the 6th Northants showed enormous courage in putting a machine gun out of action. In so doing he became the first man of his regiment to win the Victoria Cross. The official account of his action [*London Gazette*, 26th October 1916] reads:

William Ewart Boulter VC

'During the capture of Trones Wood one company and a portion of another company was held up by a machine-gun which was causing heavy casualties. Sergeant Boulter, realising the situation, with complete disregard of his personal safety and in spite of being severely wounded in the

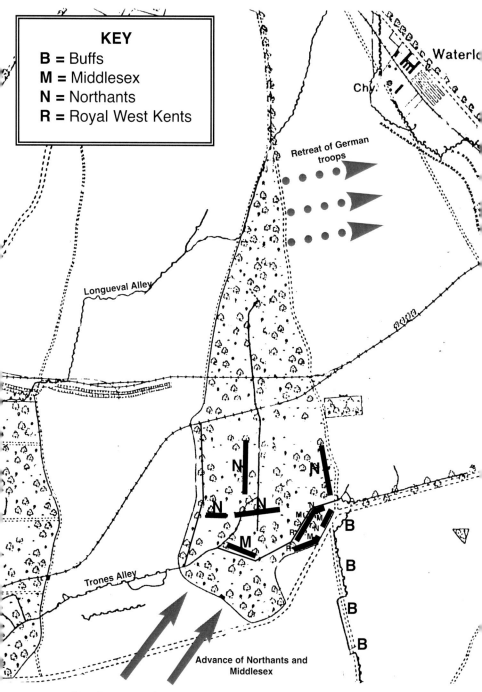

KEY

B = Buffs
M = Middlesex
N = Northants
R = Royal West Kents

Waterlo

Chy

Retreat of German troops

Longueval Alley

N N N

N N

M

B

B

Trones Alley

B

B

Advance of Northants and Middlesex

Map 7. Maxwell's troop dispositions within Trones Wood, 14th July 1916

shoulder, advanced alone across the open in front of the gun under heavy fire and bombed the team from their position, thereby saving the lives of many of his comrades and materially assisting the advance which eventually cleared Trones Wood.'

After the fighting at Trones Wood Sergeant Boulter was hospitalised in the UK until March 1917, after which he was promoted 2nd Lieutenant on 27 June 1917. Before the war William Boulter had worked in the haberdashery department of the Co-Operative Stores at Kettering. Afterwards it was said of him that it was always difficult to persuade him to describe his exploit. As a rule, all he would say was that he had with him that morning a revolver that kept going off; and so he killed Germans!

By 9.30 am, more than six hours after the attack on the German Second Position had begun, the genuine northern apex of Trones Wood was gained.

Finally the British had taken the advantage here at Trones Wood. To the east of the wood Germans had fled from the confines of its northern end where they had become trapped by Maxwell's advance. As they ran desperately towards Waterlot Farm and Guillemont and the protection of their Second Positions there these men were gunned down in great numbers by the soldiers of the Middlesex and Northampton battalions, which were now in complete control of the eastern perimeter of the wood, and by the rifles of the 7th Buffs which now controlled the strong-point on the Guillemont road.

The capture of Trones Wood secured the right flank of the advance of the 9th Division's men towards Longueval. The phrase 'better late than never' might be employed to describe the events here at Trones, but I prefer to think that 'cometh the hour – cometh the man' might be more appropriate to describe Maxwell's remarkable achievements here. Perhaps, under different circumstances he might have become the second soldier to win one of two Victoria Crosses here facing Guillemont.

Post Script. The Dawn Attack on 14th July

The capture of Trones Wood on the morning of 14th July cannot be said to have ensured that all which occurred during that day's Dawn Attack went well. Trones Wood was the scene of preliminary operations which initially went badly wrong. The cause was, as we have seen, the delays which mounted during the first week of the Somme offensive. It is, however, all too easy to say that these delays resulted in Trones Wood being left isolated when its capture could have

The scene adjacent to the southern end of Bernafay Wood looking east in the direction of Trones Wood. Supplies litter both sides of the route in this photograph taken in the mid summer of 1916.
Below: The same stretch of road today.

been effected without great loss. The reality is that Trones Wood could certainly have been captured on the 3rd or 4th July but, just as certainly, the cost of holding it against superior artillery would have been enormous. What is true is that the final desperate attempts to

capture Trones Wood on the 13th and 14th July did divert German attention from what was happening to the west and north-west of the wood. As the four divisions assembled beneath the Longueval ridge that night the sounds of the struggle within Trones Wood's confines masked any noise which those thousands of tense soldiers made. In this context the preliminary operation to capture Trones Wood became a successful diversion and one which, at the very last moment, was certainly beneficial to the Dawn Attack's chances of success.

In effecting the wood's capture on 14th July the 18th (Eastern) Division proved itself to be a highly competent and formidable fighting force. Maxse's reputation as an effective organiser was greatly enhanced. His New Army division's fighting reputation was then ensured. That it would be used on a number of further occasions when lesser divisions were rejected as unsuitable was inevitable.

The Dawn Attack on the Longueval to Bazentin-le-Petit ridge was a

A break for officers of the Manchesters after fighting in the area leading to Guillemont.

triumph. The most significant factor in the morning's success was the forward and silent deployment of the assault troops in No Man's Land, in readiness for the attack. North of Bernafay Wood and east of Trones Wood it was the soldiers of the 9th (Scottish) Division who were able to benefit from the capture of Trones, moving the British front forward from the northern perimeter of Bernafay into Longueval village. Adjacent to the site of Longueval Road cemetery[10] the 8th Black Watch had been chosen as the right flank unit at the eastern end of this massive assembly of men. The fact that this assembly and assault was carried out under the most arduous and dangerous circumstances, almost exclusively by other New Army troops, meant that its innovative methodology would forever be used as a point in argument to suggest that, had similar tactics been possible, on the morning of 1 July the great disaster which befell the British could have been avoided.[11] However, the purpose of this book is not to address that question – but now to consider the course of the fighting for the village of Guillemont, in the German main Second Position, to the east of Trones Wood.

1. On your IGN maps Maltz Horn Valley is denoted as the 'Fond des Maras'. The valley's trench map reference is sheet 62cNW1, A5b and A6a. The very upper limit of Maltz Horn Valley is found on sheet 57cSW3, S30c and it is this map which also covers the Trones Wood – Longueval – Guillemont area. Maltz Horn Valley was sometimes referred to in contemporary British accounts as 'Death Valley'.
2. That attack eventually took place, very succesfully from the British perspective, on the morning of 14th July.
3. *Military Operations. France and Belgium. 1916.* Vol 2. pp 43.
4. From 9th Division. The 9th (Scottish) Division consisted of 26 and 27 Brigade as well as the South African Brigade. Amongst the South Africans the 4th Regiment was known as the 'Scottish'.
5. Located at 57cSW3, S,30,a,5,4.
6. A full and detailed account of these events can be found in; *18th Division in the Great War*, G.H.F.Nichols, Blackwood & Sons, 1922.
7. Located at 57cSW3, S,24,c,4,0.
8. Maxwell had won the VC whilst serving in South Africa. He later served as Kitchener's ADC. During September 1916 he was instrumental in the 18th Division's succesful attempts to complete the capture of Thiepval. Undoubtedly a fine and brave officer, Maxwell was killed at Third Ypres whilst commanding 27 Brigade.
9. *18th Division in the Great War*, pp 64/65.
10. Next to the cemetery a small shrine is the subject of local legend which suggests that Julius Caesar addressed one of his legions here during the Roman subjection of Gaul.
11. On 1 July a night time assembly was not an option for the British since the French wanted a 7.30 am attack, and had originally wanted it even later in the day.

Chapter Four

THE BATTLES FOR GUILLEMONT VILLAGE

Part 1. July and August 1916

Before the war Guillemont village had a relatively unprepossessing place in the life of the Somme region. Its main thoroughfare, the Rue d'En-Bas, was the backdrop for a typical collection of Somme farm building and dwellings. Numerous agricultural implements, ploughs, harrows and seed drills littered the street. The centre of the village was a rather gaudy church whose architecture seemed rooted in inappropriate style for such an agrarian and tranquil backwater.

Guillemont's topography and location would not lead you to suppose that it could provide a thorn in the side of British progress well into the third month of the Somme battles. Guillemont stood at the shallow head of Caterpillar Valley which wound its way from Fricourt, past Mametz Wood and then the northern end of Bernafay Wood into Trones Wood. By this stage in the valley's course it is of little

The Rue d'En-Bas, Guillemont's main street, in pre-war days. [Reed]

significance but the upper reaches of the valley, noted as the Vallee du Bois des Troncs on your IGN map, are quite discernible to the left of the Guillemont road as you look from the east of Trones Wood towards Guillemont village. On the immediate left of the roadside stands the impressive portal of the Guillemont Road Cemetery which is a fine location from which to view this area of the Somme battlefield. There is little difference in elevation between Guillemont and Trones Wood. The south-eastern tip of the wood stands at 142 metres above sea level – Guillemont's elevation exceeding that by one metre! The more dominant locations, in terms of elevation in this vicinity, are Ginchy at 154 metres and Delville Wood at 156 metres. But Guillemont's interest lies in

Guillemont church, photographed during the German occupation in the winter of 1915-16. By the late July of 1916 the structure had vanished into pulverised brick dust and rubble. [Reed]

the fact that it is located towards the south-eastern end of the great Thiepval - Pozieres ridge whose lesser spurs run down through the Ginchy - Guillemont area as they lose height towards Hardecourt and, eventually, the River Somme.

Once Trones Wood had been secured on 14 July there now elapsed a period of some days before conditions favourable to the chances of a successful assault on Guillemont were created. Although only a short distance from Trones Wood any attempt to capture it at the start of the third week of fighting would only have served to make even more prominent a British salient in the Waterlot Farm – Longueval area. Any attempt to capture Guillemont would also have suffered from enfilade fire directed from Delville Wood to the north-west and it was therefore deemed essential that at least those parts of Longueval and Delville

Wood which overlooked Guillemont be in British hands before the attack on Guillemont was undertaken. During this time the focus of the British efforts on the Somme battlefront were therefore directed against Longueval and Delville Wood together with High Wood and the Pozieres defences.

One of the first and most pressing tasks to secure the left flank of any attack upon Guillemont lay at Waterlot Farm. In pre war years this dominant structure had been a sugar refinery. Now, in the centre of the most enormous conflagration the world had yet witnessed, the fallen brickwork of its many buildings, its extensive cellars and earthworks had been developed by the Germans as a feature of their main Second Position, a little way south-east of Longueval on the road towards Guillemont. At dawn on 15 July an attack was made down this road by a company of the 5th Cameron Highlanders, later supplemented by two companies of the 4th South African Regiment. After fierce fighting the Germans were driven out but it proved quite impossible to maintain a hold on the refinery in view of the terrible and intense shelling which was then poured into its confines by the Germans. Not until 17 July was Waterlot Farm finally consolidated into British control.

The main road into Guillemont. The shattered trees are those flanking the route from Waterlot Farm to Guillemont, clearly shown on the contemporary trench maps. This photograph was taken in September, soon after Guillemont's capture.

Private Clifford Hicks, 17th Lancashire Fusiliers, a soldier from the 35th (Bantam) Division. His brigade, 104, consisted of men raised in south Lancashire and Manchester. Clifford Hicks survived the war. For the rest of his life (he died aged 74 in 1970) he could never speak of the horrors he witnessed at Trones Wood or Guillemont. [Hartley]

A mere stone's throw to the north-west, throughout this period, the South Africans were engaged in the most desperate fighting for Delville Wood. That fighting replicated many of the circumstances which had made the capture of Trones Wood such a misery. Nevertheless, on 17th July an important conference was held at Dury, where Rawlinson and General Foch met to discuss the immediate future of combined operations in the Somme area. It was agreed that Guillemont and Ginchy be attacked by the British on the 19th, and that the following day the whole German front between Falfemont Farm[1] and the Somme be subjected to a combined Franco-British attack. Guillemont, it was anticipated, would therefore become the scene of a preliminary attack, undertaken by the British, to secure a more general and combined advance planned to the south. In the event this plan came to nought in the grip of bad weather and the exhaustion which had set in amidst those divisions which had been committed throughout the first three weeks of the attacks on the Somme. One extraordinary example of such endurance was the 18th Division which was still located in positions around Trones Wood, Maltz Horn Farm trench and the Briqueterie having first been engaged almost three weeks before, during their assault towards Pommiers Redoubt and Caterpillar Wood. On the night of 18 July the 18th Division were relieved from their locations around Trones Wood and Maltz Horn Trench by the 35th Division – the Bantams.

At this time both Haig and Rawlinson were worried that any successful German counter attack from the Longueval positions would place in jeopardy the many British batteries which were now

British stretcher bearers bring in the wounded amongst many German prisoners of war. This scene was photographed on 19th July in Bernafay Wood close to the dressing stations located there. Note the water cart being manhandled by the German prisoners. Sufficient fresh water supplies were an on going problem for the British.

concentrated within Caterpillar Valley. On 19 July Rawlinson, in consultation with General Fayolle and General Foch, therefore agreed that the British and French would attack, simultaneously on 23 July, all German main Second Positions from Waterlot Farm to the River Somme.

20 July saw the Bantams in action to cover the advance of the French who were expected to make a major effort this day, astride both banks of the Somme. In fact there was no discernible French movement on the Bantam's right, but the Bantams nevertheless stuck to their task, which was the capture of German trenches between Maltz Horn Farm and Arrow Head Copse. Arrow Head Copse lay a little east of Trones Wood, south of the Guillemont road (at 57cSW3, S,30,b,3,3). The purpose behind this attack by the Bantams was to create a more advantageous position from which the general attack upon Guillemont and the German Second Position could be launched. The Bantam's attack resulted in no progress and 450 casualties from concentrated machine-gun, rifle and shell fire. However, further south the French did achieve some progress, reaching the western slopes of the Maurepas ravine beyond Hardecourt as well as the station on the Hardecourt – Maurepas road and further south-eastwards towards the River Somme.

See German map page 154

Waterlot Farm

Sta.

Cemetery

Guillemont

Trônes Wood

Arrow Head Copse

Map 7 Detail from the 1:10,000 trench map (corrected to 24/7/1916) showing the Trones Wood – Arrow Head Copse – Guillemont area in detail.

Therefore, at this stage, 20th July, the British front line facing Guillemont was still located on the eastern perimeter of Trones Wood down to Maltz Horn Farm, although beyond the northern tip of the wood's wreckage the front line swung north-eastwards towards Waterlot Farm. On the 21st the 17th Lancashire Fusiliers replaced another bantam unit, the 18th Lancashire Fusiliers, in these front lines. A measure of the severity with which the Germans were shelling these positions can be gauged from the casualties which the 17/LFs suffered during the period 21-24 July during which they simply garrisoned the front lines without making any attacks; five officers wounded, 32 other ranks killed, 147 wounded and 2 missing[2]. The parts of Delville Wood under British control, and Waterlot Farm, therefore existed as a pronounced and insecure salient in the British lines. Rawlinson's hope was that progress past Ginchy, Guillemont and Falfemont Farm would straighten the British lines, removing the insecurity of the Delville Wood – Waterlot Farm salient and securing the safety of those many batteries exposed in Caterpillar Valley.

French participation in the plan to capture Guillemont and Falfemont Farm on 23 July was extensive. Their artillery was to be deployed to destroy the Falfemont Farm defences before its occupation by British troops. XIII Corps would assault the whole line between Waterlot and Falfemont farms, the German main Second Position, in close co-operation with the attack of the French XX Corps on its left and the British XV Corps on its left. The reality proved very different in the complexity of arranging what Rawlinson, Congreve (XIII Corps) and Horne (XV Corps) hoped would be a general attack timed to coincide with the Gough's Reserve Army's attack on Pozieres as well! On 22 July the French announced that they could not be ready for their part in this enormous enterprise until 24 July at the earliest. As a consequence the plans of XIII Corps were scaled down and it was decided that, on the right, the 30th Division would capture Guillemont whilst on the left a further attempt was to be made to complete the capture of Delville Wood by the 3rd Division. It is worth noting here that the 3rd Division's objectives stretched from Longueval and Delville Wood all the way south-east to Guillemont Station and it was therefore unfortunate that, at such a crucial location, the impetus of the attack should be complicated by the conjunction of these two divisions.

As a preliminary to the assault on Guillemont, now due at 3.40 am on Sunday 23 July, attempts were made on the 22nd to secure more advantageous positions for those attacks to be made the following day by the 3rd and 30th Division's men. At 1.30 am the 35th Division made

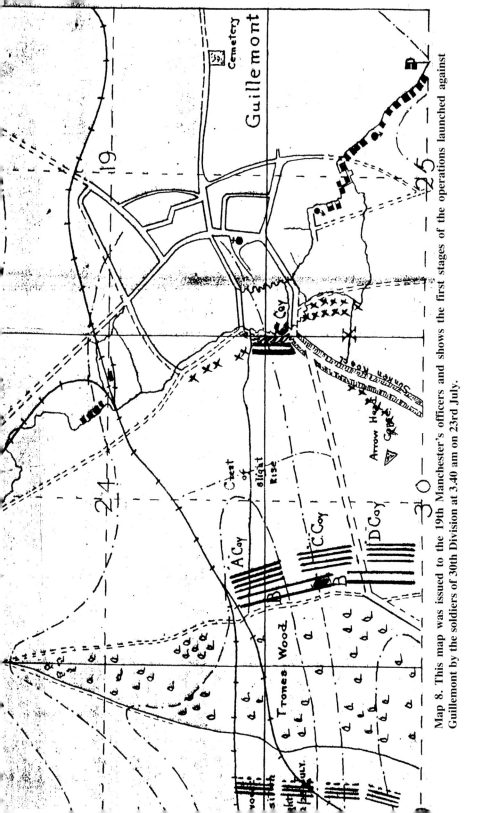

Map 8. This map was issued to the 19th Manchester's officers and shows the first stages of the operations launched against Guillemont by the soldiers of 30th Division at 3.40 am on 23rd July.

another unsuccessful attempt to carry the German trenches between Maltz Horn Farm and Arrow Head Copse, whilst half an hour later men of the 3rd Division also attempted the capture of Guillemont railway station (located at S,24,d,8,9) by attack from Waterlot Farm. The 3rd Division's men were forced back under a hail of machine-gun fire.

23rd July's attacks against Guillemont village

On the morning of the 23rd attacks on Guillemont were undertaken by units of the 30th Division from the direction of Waterlot Farm and also from the northern segment of Trones Wood above the railway line's point of exit on its eastern perimeter.

The reason why these attacks were developed from the direction of Waterlot Farm and the northern end of Trones Wood was simply to avoid the wide expanse of open and exposed glacis due west of Guillemont (in the vicinity of what is now the Guillemont Road Cemetery). The 19th Manchesters (4th Pals) were the key unit and their attack was supported on their left by the 2nd Green Howards. The 19th Manchesters' attack was preceded by a massive artillery bombardment. Apart from devastating the village, and its trenches being manned by the 104th Reserve Regiment's men, the heavy guns also placed standing barrages on the eastern side of the village, the southern end of Leuze Wood, the southern face of Ginchy village, Wedge Wood and Falfemont Farm – all places which might provide the cover for German reinforcements to assemble within and advance from. A further protection was to be derived from a barrage on the flank south of Arrow Head Copse. The barrage on the village itself was due to lift through the village in four stages, coming to rest on the eastern and southern limits forty five minutes after zero.

The 19th Manchesters attacked from the eastern perimeter of Trones Wood with three companies in line. Only when the men reached the German wire did they realise that it was uncut. After forcing the wire the Manchesters then entered the village and were immediately engulfed in very fierce fighting. Some parties of the Manchesters got as far as the eastern limits[3] where they initially surrounded the battle headquarters of the III/104th Reserve Regiment. However, those men who penetrated furthest eventually found themselves cut off and those who could do so were eventually forced to withdraw. No reinforcements were able to cross the area of No Man's Land west of Guillemont and the attack failed as the 19th Manchesters were gradually exhausted. On the left of the Manchesters the attack of the 2nd Green Howards, made from Longueval Alley, was a shambles, the men being confused by their own smoke barrage which was blown across their path by a northerly wind! Some groups of the Green Howards crossed the advance of the Manchesters and found themselves against uncut wire south-west of Guillemont before falling back to Trones Wood. Others from the Green Howards' attack did manage to capture a trench just south of the railway line but were themselves ejected and forced to fall back towards Waterlot Farm where the 2nd Green Howards' men then managed to disorganise the attacks being made by the 3rd Division. It was a sorry tale.

That part of the 3rd Division's assault, directed south-eastwards down the Longueval to Guillemont road, known as High Holborn, on Guillemont Station failed to make a secure advance and the men were also forced back into the Waterlot Farm area.

This failure to capture Guillemont on 23 July now meant that there was a large question mark hanging over the prospect of any joint Anglo - French attack north of the River Somme. Undaunted, at 6.15 pm on the 23rd, Rawlinson issued further instructions for the continuance of operations. XIII Corps' orders continued in exactly the same vein as before: clear Longueval and Delville Wood, in conjunction with the next French attack north of the Somme and to assault the German main Second Positions between Falfemont Farm and Guillemont inclusive. For the village of Guillemont that meant another pause until the events of 30 July.

General Sir Henry Rawlinson

The events of 30th July in the Guillemont area

Overnight on the 29/30th July the 30th Division's soldiers were again moved up to positions in the Trones Wood – Maltz Horn Trench area. The plan envisaged that these men would attack through the 35th (Bantam) Division's men who were still garrisoning the front lines[4]. Whilst the 30th Division was being brought forward in darkness the

See German maps page 155 and 156

68

Private C.W. Cope, X Platoon, C Coy, 18th Manchesters. Private Cope was killed near Guillemont on 30 July. His body was found, somewhere between the northern end of Trones Wood and the Station, by a burial party belonging to the 1/4th Loyal North Lancs. In a letter dated 5 August 1916 one of the party, Private J. Collier, wrote to Private Cope's family:

'Dear Friend,

Please excuse me writing to you, as I am the sender of very bad news, I am extremely sorry to inform you of the death of Private C. Cope. I do not know him personally but me and a chum of mine were out burying the dead and we found him lying in a shell hole, by the look of him he could not have suffered no pain, so we paid the best respects we could and buried him.'

Like many similar burials that simple grave was never located after Guillemont's final capture and Private Cope's name is now inscribed, along with many others from his regiment, on the Thiepval Memorial to the Missing.

[Alexander/Davis]

German barrage on Trones Wood increased in intensity and a number of the units were very badly affected by both gas and high explosive shells. Zero hour was set for 4.45 am but as dawn broke it was apparent that thick fog had reduced visibility to less than forty yards. However, the attack was launched with 89 Brigade's objective as Falfemont Farm and the German lines north-west to Guillemont and 90 Brigade's objectives as Guillemont village. Guillemont Station, and the trenches north-west of it towards Waterlot Farm, was to be carried by 5 Brigade of the 2nd Division.

In the murk of the mist which lay thick in every hollow Maltz Horn Farm was captured and some men of the 20th King's then reached the Hardecourt – Guillemont road. In Guillemont soldiers of the 2nd Royal Scots had advanced along the Trones Wood to Guillemont road and entered the village, taking many prisoners. The Royal Scots were then joined by the 18th Manchesters who had moved forward from the eastern side of Trones Wood towards the northern half of the village. This attack was given fresh impetus by the support of both the 16th and

CSM George Evans, VC.

17th Manchesters but again no secure lodgement within the northern portion of the village could be achieved. The soldiers confined within the Guillemont locality were now in great danger of being cut off. Many German counter attacks in the area were being developed and runners, attempting to convey reports to brigade and battalion HQs in Trones Wood were being shot down after the fog began to clear at 9.00 am. It was in this context that CSM George Evans of the 18th Manchesters won his VC for his gallantry in delivering messages[5].

Gradually the 19th King's began to succumb to the pressure of German counter attacks on the south of Guillemont and were forced to pull back. The British artillery was faced with the dilemma of what to do about the 2nd Royal Scots in Guillemont itself. In the event the village was not shelled and the Royal Scots fought on, unsupported, until they were all killed or captured.

Further north the attacks made by the 2nd Division were a failure and the troops were eventually withdrawn to their assembly positions. The only gains from the events was the capture of the trench leading from Arrow Head Copse along the sunken part of the Guillemont to Hardecourt road to Maltz Horn Farm where the right flank of the 30th Division was in touch with the French. The losses of the units had been depressingly heavy. In 89 Brigade those losses amounted to 1,314 casualties. 90 Brigade lost 1,463. The 2nd Royal Scots had been virtually wiped out, losing 17 officers and 633 other ranks, comparable with the losses of almost any unit engaged on day one of the Somme battles.

The outcome of 30 July's attacks had almost exactly mirrored those which preceded them on 23 July. Guillemont was simply a very strongly defended location surrounded by an open glacis, utterly devoid of cover both to the west of the village and over the Maltz Horn knoll to the south-west of the village. The depth of dug-outs and the many interconnected tunnels meant that any limited British infantry advance into the village could then be isolated and dealt with as the German defenders emerged to take these units in the rear. The British front line facing Guillemont was still the eastern perimeter of Trones Wood. As day ended XIII Corps commander, Lieutenant General

Congreve, relieved all the forward troops of the 35th and 30th Divisions and replaced them with the newly arrived 55th Division's men[6].

The events of August 1916

More than four weeks into the campaign the German Second Positions at Guillemont still held firm. Haig was adamant that the fight be continued, but that the present stage of operations should be regarded as a 'wearing out' battle in which subsequent operations should only be delivered using the greatest economy of men and material so that, as the Official History so succinctly put it: 'the Allies should have at their disposal the 'Last Reserves' when the crisis of the fighting was reached.'

Even so, the first instinct of Haig and Rawlinson was to help the French Sixth Army get forward by securing the positions at Guillemont, Ginchy and Falfemont Farm. Whilst the French did attack on 7 August it proved impossible to make comparable arrangements for Congreve's XIII Corps, especially the 55th Division, who were hampered greatly by the strength of artillery which the Germans used to oppose every move opposite Guillemont. However, the 55th Division's men used every opportunity during the first week of August to dig preparatory trenches sufficiently forward to bring them to within assaulting distance of the German positions around the Station and the western limits of the village. The 55th Division's attacks on Guillemont would start on 8 August in tandem with attacks made by the 2nd Division between Waterlot Farm and the northern end of Guillemont by the Station. During 7 August a number of feints were carried out by the artillery simulating the final preparations for an assault by the infantry. The purpose of these feints was to keep the German defenders on edge and in doubt as to when and where the final attack would occur.

There was really no need for such subterfuge. The final barrage would leave no one in doubt as to when, where or how the assault on Guillemont would occur. The artillery plan was similar to all those which had been employed during July's failed attacks. Throughout 7 August the artillery feints continued, and on the 8th the heavy artillery of XIII Corps lifted from the German front lines fifteen minutes before zero at 4.20 am, and began to pound the trenches cutting across the centre of the village. The morning was characteristically misty with very limited visibility. Twenty minutes later the heavy artillery would lift towards the village's eastern limits. Thereafter the heavy guns

71

would place a standing barrage on positions east of Guillemont around Wedge Wood, on the slopes between Ginchy and Guillemont and finally in front of Leuze Wood. The divisional field guns would concentrate their fire on Guillemont village, lifting through the village in five stages, ten minutes apart on each lift.

Amongst the infantry the most elaborate preparation were made to keep every member of each unit fully informed as to his role. That perhaps begs the question as to whether or not individual soldiers were denied such information in earlier attacks. Whatever, there was a huge depth of support made available to every unit, contact planes to spot the advance, ground flares, mirrors, lamps and even a radio station in a trench north-east of Faviere Wood. But just to keep within the norms for the time pigeons were taken forward and the men were obliged to wear reflective tin discs on their back as a further aid to observers.

As soon as the attack got underway all the men disappeared from view in a dense cloud of dank mist, smoke and dust. The German barrage began to search No Man's Land and for an hour and a half no news of the attack was heard at the 55th Division's HQ. In that time some progress was made by the men of 1/5th King's (165 Brigade) across the spur east of Maltz Horn Farm to the south of Guillemont. Unfortunately this advance proved to have no substance in that it was unsupported on either flank. It nevertheless represented the sole British gain of the day. On the left of the 1/5th King's the 1/4th King's Own (164 Brigade) was repulsed at the wire on the south-west corner of the village. Although these men bravely tried to dig in, almost within bombing range of the German defenders, they were eventually forced to retire to their assembly trenches. It was during this action that 2nd Lieutenant Gabriel Coury of the 1/4th South Lancashires, the 55th Division's Pioneer battalion, would win the Victoria Cross.

Gabriel George Coury was born on 13 June, 1896, at Sefton Park, Liverpool, son of Raphael and Marie Coury, of Liverpool. His father was a cotton merchant. He was educated at Stonyhurst College, where he won many prizes for sports, before being apprenticed to one of the many cotton firms in that area. He joined the Army in August 1914, as a private in the 6th King's. Coury was given a commission in the 3rd Battalion The Prince of Wales's Volunteers (South Lancashire Regiment) in April, 1915; then served in the 4th South Lancs until August 1916 from which he joined the RFC as an observer, returning to England in May, 1917. He was promoted Lieutenant on 8 August 1916, and Captain during September 1918. He was awarded the Victoria Cross [*London Gazette*, 26 Oct.1916]; Gabriel George Coury,

Bringing up an 18 pounder during the attack.

Lieutenant (then Second Lieutenant), 3rd Battalion, The Prince of Wales's Volunteers (South Lancashire Regiment).

2nd Lieutenant Gabriel George Coury. VC

'For most conspicuous bravery. During an advance he was in command of two platoons ordered to dig a communication trench from the old firing line to the position won. By his fine example and utter contempt of danger he kept up the spirits of his men, and completed his task under intense fire. Later, after his battalion had suffered severe casualties and the commanding officer had been wounded, he went out in front of the advanced position in broad daylight, and in full view of the enemy found his commanding officer and brought him back to the new advanced trench over ground swept by machine-gun fire. He not only carried out his original task, and saved his commanding officer, but also assisted in rallying the attacking troops when they were shaken and in leading them forward.'

The officer referred to within the citation was Major J.L.Swainson, commanding officer of the 1/4th Kings Own, 164 Brigade, who had been wounded during the earlier attacks.

The difficulty which all the assaults on Guillemont were labouring under was the inability of the British artillery to locate and destroy the many machine-gun nests scattered within the wreckage of the village. Whilst the German machine gunners retained the will to continue, and the British artillery failed to winkle out these astonishingly resilient and brave men, the machine gun continued to dominate the Guillemont battlefield. In reality the subterranean tunnels made the artillery's task an impossible one. Typical of the circumstances this day was the fate which befell the 1st King's. This battalion was attacking towards The Station, Brompton Road and High Holborn and the position known as Machine Gun House.[7] The King's soldiers had been lying out in the open before advancing at 4.20 am. In the dense cloud of dust and smoke the men had gone too far south, missing the strong points around the station and only entering High Holborn via the confines of Brompton Road, although almost immediately the Germans had then re-occupied their front line from their still intact dug-outs and tunnels.

When the three attacking companies, B, C and D were later supported by A Company this last company was therefore met by heavy machine gun fire and a shower of grenades as they tried to approach the German front lines. Nevertheless, by 5.20 flares signalled

74

that Guillemont had been captured and Lieutenant Colonel Charles Goff of the 1st King's sent back the news, by pigeon, that:

'First, we have taken front line and station and I think High Holborn. Everything is rather mixed. Machine guns are firing at us from Guillemont and from our left. I am at present in German front line and am going forward to clear up the situation.'

The words are so typical of the laconic style and immense bravery which personified the Regular soldier's approach to his duty. They are Goff's last testimony since he was soon to be killed along with his second-in-command, Major McErvel, and many of the battalion's subalterns and men.

South of the 1st King's the situation in Guillemont had been changed by an inspirational attack made by the 1/8th King's, the Liverpool Irish, 164 Brigade, who fought their way into Guillemont past both sides of the quarry. Problematically the situation could not be made secure and a company of the 1/4th Loyal North Lancs who were sent up to hold the old German front line behind the 1/8th King's men, were bombed out of it by counter attack from the south, thus isolating the 1/8th King's within the village. That counter attack also ensured the Germans' success in cutting off the 1st Battalion's men, who were thus

Guillemont village showing the total destruction by British shellfire. Entrances to tunnels made by the Germans, and which ran under the village and surrounding areas, connecting wells and providing shelter, can be discerned.

also trapped. Worse, the German machine-guns were now sweeping the original No-Man's-Land west of Guillemont making any communication with, or reinforcement of, the King's an impossibility. The whole of the 2nd Division's attack, of which the 1st King's were a small part, being made both from Trones Wood north of the light railway line and from the north-west from Waterlot Farm, was therefore foundering again in the area of Guillemont Station. Within this maelstrom of death the King's regiment now had both a regular and territorial unit within the confines of the village. The other units of the 2nd and 55th Divisions forward of Trones Wood had a very tough time during these exchanges. Crowded into assembly trenches, suffering an intense artillery bombardment, uncertain of the outcome to the east, these men took heavy casualties whilst frozen in a state of suspended activity.

Although orders were issued by XIII Corps for these units to advance to the support of the 1st and 1/8th Kings it proved impossible within the confines of such chaotically overcrowded trenches to organise such movements on the 8th. Eventually Congreve ordered the two divisions to replicate their attack the following morning, 9 August, at 4.20 am, with the same objectives. Whilst this process of organising further attacks went ahead the mixed units of the King's regiment fought on within Guillemont until, 36 hours after their initial attack, the remnants were killed or captured at the quarry and later fighting in the vicinity of the Station[8]. 164 Brigade's diary records that the nature of the problem was now understood.

'As soon as they had got into the village it appears that the enemy came up out of the ground below them and cut them off entirely by means of machine guns. This is practically what happened on the previous attack on Guillemont on 30th July, and it is possible that the village is an underground warren of passages in which the garrison is immune from shell fire, and from which they can emerge with their machine guns after the attacking infantry has passed over.'

Interestingly the date 8 August marks one of those few moments when Haig's hold on his command might have wavered. On this morning the monarch travelled to France, lunching at GHQ in Montreuil before driving to meet with Haig at Beauquesne, Haig's advanced HQ. The King, who was well disposed towards Haig and his style of leadership, wanted to discuss Winston Churchill's[9] critique of the Somme Offensive which had given rise to disturbing questions amongst the Cabinet's membership. The events at Guillemont during the previous month were a perfect example of why Churchill's concerns had surfaced. Haig was fortunate that the King was so well attuned to the Commander-in-Chief's thinking. In fact, as events in London unfolded this day, the C.I.G.S, Sir William Robertson, sent a message to Haig 'assuring him that he might count on full support from home.'

However, back at Guillemont, on the morning of 9 August, the replica attack was made, again at 4.20 am, by those men of the 2nd and 55th Divisions who had now been exposed to ordeal by shellfire for the best part of two days in their trenches within and south-west of Trones Wood. Many of the men were in a desperate state, unfed and short of sleep, dazed by the constant detonations which seemed to accompany their every move. The whole area surrounding Trones Wood and Guillemont was now infested with a haze of fat flies, bluebottles, whose maggots gnawed at the wounds of any man lying out in the open for any lengthy period of time. One unit whose actions this morning deserve close scrutiny is the 1/10th King's, the Liverpool Scottish, whose men tried desperately to close with the German defenders on the left of the 55th Division's advance.

During the night of 8/9 August the Liverpool Scottish had moved up from their reserve positions, moving past the south of Trones Wood towards Arrow Head Copse. The journey had been very difficult. No guides had turned up and when replacements finally did arrive their knowledge of the route proved sketchy. Eventually 166 Brigade's men were in place, astride the Trones Wood to Guillemont road. On the right, south of the road, were the 1/10th King's with the 5th Loyal North Lancs on their left to the north of the road. The Liverpool Scots had been granted just minutes to prepare themselves for the attack and the men's sense of direction and familiarity with the terrain was not firmly grounded. The bombardment which preceded their advance was weak and, as soon as the men rose to advance, they were met by seemingly unsupressed machine-gun fire. In these terrifying circumstances the attack was constantly rallied by Lieutenant Colonel Davidson, his battalion making four charges in all, each to no avail. Amongst the Liverpool Scots the casualties were heavy. Five officers killed, five more missing, seven wounded, 69 men killed, 27 missing and 167 wounded.

This action was the scene for those events surrounding the winning of the Victoria Cross by Noel Chavasse, the 1/10th King's inspirational medical officer. During the day he watched three of the battalion's doomed charges. That evening Captain Noel Chavasse took a group of his stretcher bearers out into No Man's Land in front of Guillemont and began the process of trying to identify the dead and succour the wounded. Throughout the night Chavasse's team worked on, inspired by his cool and good natured manner. As he searched the shattered terrain Chavasse brought his characteristic qualities of humanity and dedication to the gruesome task in hand. Eventually dawn forced abandonment and Chavasse returned, later to find that he had been wounded. His words on the subject were the epitome of his typically reticent understatement. '...the merest particle of shell just frisked me. I did not even know about it till I undressed at night.'[10]

The subsequent citation, published in the London Gazette on 26th October 1916, spoke in fine terms of the dignified and determined valour which Noel Chavasse had shown whilst carrying out his duties.

'During an attack he tended the wounded in the open all day, under heavy fire, frequently in view of the enemy. During the ensuing night he searched for wounded on the ground in front of the enemy's lines for four hours. Next day he took one stretcher-bearer to the advanced trenches, and, under heavy fire, carried an urgent case for 500 yards into safety, being wounded in the side by a shell splinter during the journey. The same night he took up a party of trusty volunteers, rescued three wounded men from a shell-hole twenty-five yards from the enemy's trench, buried the bodies of two officers, and collected many identity discs, although fired on by bombs and machine guns. Altogether he saved the lives of some twenty badly wounded men, besides the ordinary cases which passed through his hands. His courage and self-sacrifice were beyond praise.'

One important post war publication, *The Victoria Cross 1856-1920*, written by Sir O'Moore Creagh, devotes a great deal of space to biographical details covering Chavasse's life. I have reproduced some of that below in a rather condensed manner:

Noel Godfrey Chavasse, M.B., Captain, born at Oxford, 9 Nov 1884, son of the Right Reverend The Lord Bishop of Liverpool and of Edith Jane Chavasse, daughter of Canon Maude, Rector of Chirk. He was twin brother to the Reverend C. M. Chavasse, M.C., Temporary Chaplain to the Forces. Noel Chavasse was educated at Magdalen College School (1896-1900), Liverpool College School (1900-1904), and at Trinity College Oxford (1904-1908), and was a well-known athlete. Chavasse ran in athletic contests for Oxford against Cambridge, both in 1907 and 1908. In the former year he ran a dead-heat in the 100 yards with K.G. Macleod in under 11 seconds, and was second to his twin brother, C.M.Chavasse, in the quarter mile. Noel was not so successful in 1908, rupturing a thigh muscle in the hundred yards. However, he also represented Oxford at Lacrosse, both in 1904-5 and 1905-6. Capt. Chavasse was a Medical Officer at the Royal Southern Hospital, Liverpool, before the war. He joined the Royal Army Medical Corps in 1913, being attached to the 10th (Liverpool Scottish) King's Own, and served with them in the European War in France. He was awarded the Military Cross before being awarded the Victoria Cross for gallantry at Guillemont. Noel Chavasse was subsequently awarded a bar to the Victoria Cross [London Gazette, 14 Sept.1917]: The citation states that: 'His Majesty the King has been graciously pleased to approve of the award of the Victoria Cross to Captain Noel Godfrey Chavasse, V.C., M.C., late R.A.M.C., attached Liverpool Regiment. Though

Noel Chavasse VC and Bar

severely wounded early in the action whilst carrying a wounded soldier to the dressing station he refused to leave his post, and for two days not only continued to perform his duties but in addition went out repeatedly under heavy fire to search for and attend to the wounded who were lying out. During these searches, although practically without food during this period, worn with fatigue and faint with his wound, he assisted to carry in a number of badly wounded men over heavy and difficult ground. By his extraordinary energy and inspiring example he was instrumental in rescuing many wounded who would have otherwise undoubtedly succumbed under the bad weather conditions. This devoted and gallant officer subsequently died of his wounds.

At a memorial service in Liverpool which was conducted by Archdeacon Spooner, Canon Lancelot gave an address. Alluding to the late Captain Noel Chavasse, V.C., he said it was no wonder that the King felt that the whole Army would mourn the death of so brave and distinguished a brother, that his Brigadier declared him to have been the most gallant and modest man he had ever

*met, that the Major-General commanding the Division should
say that his devotion was magnificent, or that the whole
battalion, smothered in mud as they were, and ready to drop from
exhaustion, paraded for his funeral. Captain Chavasse might
have been a great surgeon, or a really great clergyman and
medical missionary.'*

It would be inappropriate for me to add further to such a tribute or
commentary.

The 2nd Division's attacks against the north of the village and the
station on this day, 9 August, were again a failure.

Further Plans for Guillemont

By 9 August Haig was expressing concern about the strain which
events at Waterlot Farm, Guillemont and elsewhere on the battlefront
were placing on the staff of XIII Corps. The Corps commander's son,
the inspirational Billy Congreve VC, DSO, MC, had been killed before
High Wood the previous month. Accordingly, on 10 August, Lieutenant
General Congreve relinquished his command, being replaced by
Lieutenant General the Earl of Cavan. Cavan brought with him the
staff of XIV Corps and from midnight on 16/17 August the old XIII
Corps was renamed the XIVth. However, before Congreve departed,
his immediate superior Rawlinson had agreed with General Fayolle of
the French Sixth Army that there would be a combined attack on 11th,
the French attacking Maurepas whilst XIII Corps secured the rising
ground on the spur south of Guillemont. In the event this attack was
postponed until 12 August on the grounds of inclement weather.
Subsequently, Guillemont and Maurepas would then be attacked and
captured as soon as both armies were sure this could be achieved.
Meanwhile all units were ordered to work forward to their objectives
by: '..digging, by the seizure of enemy posts, and by advancing their
lines towards the enemy whenever an opportunity occurred.'[11] This was
the most unimaginative siege warfare. One of Congreve's last
contributions to the events at Guillemont was to report to Rawlinson,
on the morning of 10 August, that XIII Corps would be ready to
capture the village on 17 August.

During the late afternoon of the 12 August, amidst fine hot weather,
the 55th Division attempted another attack on the Maltz Horn knoll
south of Guillemont. The objective was to secure the higher ground on
the Guillemont to Hardecourt road (from east of Maltz Horn Farm at
62cNW1, B.1.a.5,5 northwards to 57cSW3, T.25.c.4,9 and thence to
S.30.b.6,1) in order to ensure that further frontal attacks on the village
were not exposed to enfilade fire from their right. On the left flank of

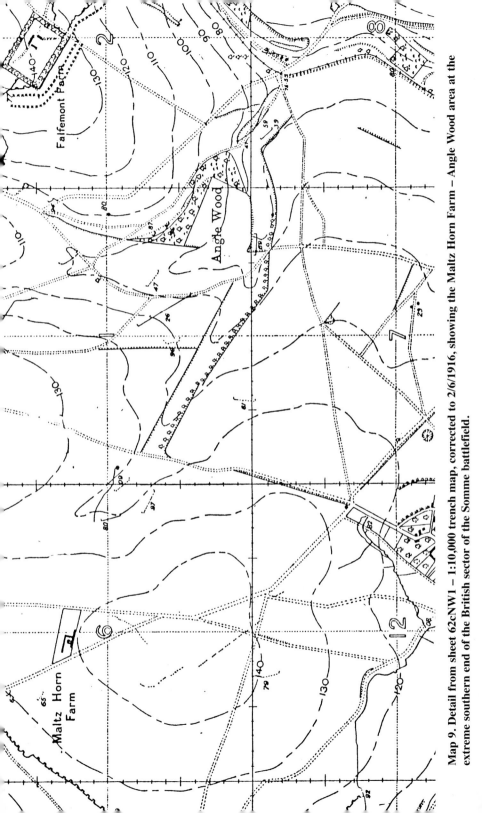

Map 9. Detail from sheet 62cNW1 – 1:10,000 trench map, corrected to 2/6/1916, showing the Maltz Horn Farm – Angle Wood area at the extreme southern end of the British sector of the Somme battlefield.

the British lines facing these positions the trenches were being held by the 1/7th King's men who heard the divisional artillery begin its bombardment at 3.30 pm. Almost immediately the German artillery fire increased in intensity. Nevertheless, the attack was made successfully at 5.15 pm under the protection of an intense bombardment. Unfortunately the expected French advance at Maurepas and the ravine failed to materialise and the 1/9th King's men who made the advance were eventually forced to withdraw since their right flank was utterly exposed. Late on 13th the King's soldiers in this vicinity were relieved.

Earlier that same day, at 10.00 am, the young Second Lieutenant Jack Fearnhead was hit, possibly by two bullets, one of which penetrated his lung. The trenches were so shallow from the devastating shelling that it proved impossible for him to be removed in daylight. The stretcher bearers of the 5th South Lancs dressed Jack's wounds whilst he was conscious, probably believing it to be superficial and promised to return that night to evacuate him. The likelihood is that the 5th South Lancs men were very hard pressed that day and Jack Fearnhead slipped into unconsciousness unnoticed. On the stretcher bearers' return he was found to be dead. Like so many other young men who were killed here at Guillemont his grave is unmarked. Jack's company commander, Captain R.G. Thompson, said in his letter of condolence that;

'They buried him on the spot, and collected his identity disc and personal belongings... I am afraid that it is not likely that the burial party will have been able to mark the grave, but it was at a spot a bare half mile south of Guillemont.'

2nd Lieutenant Jack Fearnhead. February 16th 1916. [Hall]

Further discussions about the nature of combined Franco-British operations in the area north of the Somme continued unabated. The British part of the plan was again to attempt the capture of the Hardecourt to Guillemont road before pressing forward to the northern apex of Angle Wood (located at 62cNW1, B.1.d.7,8).

On the night of 14/15 August the 55th Division was relieved of duty in the Guillemont sector. Since its arrival the division had lost over 4,100 casualties amongst all ranks. The best that the Official History could find to say about its endeavours was that 'if it had failed to capture Guillemont, [the 55th] had at least pushed forward the British right to within close assaulting distance.' In my opinion it is a sadness that the 55th Division's men have no memorial here at Guillemont. The area is littered with the unmarked graves of so many young men like Jack Fearnhead that not to mark their passing in some meaningful manner seems a tragedy in its own right. The 55th were replaced in the line by the 3rd Division whose attacks the following day were anticipated as having a good chance of success.

On 16 August the attacks were timed to occur at 5.40 pm. The weather was hot and clear, the bombardment thorough and the infantry attacks delivered punctually. All looked set for an auspicious advance. On the right the 2nd Suffolks cleared Cochrane Alley as far as the Hardecourt to Guillemont road and then bombed forward along the trench by the side of the road in the direction of Guillemont, capturing part of the trench but were unable to reach that part overlooking the south of the village. Unfortunately the isolated German position known as Lonely Trench, just west of the Hardecourt to Guillemont road, was not taken by the troops in support of the Suffolks who had to be withdrawn at nightfall. Other attacks this day directed against the north of Guillemont by the 24th Division failed, as did the French 153rd Division's attacks in the Maurepas – Angle Wood area to the right of the 3rd Division.

The strain was intolerable and the following day Lord Cavan, who had just succeeded to the corps command, was himself obliged to quit because of ill health. Cavan was replaced by Moreland who had been commanding X Corps. That evening the British front lines west of Lonely Trench were cleared in order to facilitate a heavy howitzer bombardment of the Lonely Trench area. Two hours after that had ceased a surprise attack by the 10th Royal Welsh Fusiliers and the 12th West Yorkshires failed to get in. Six hours later another attempt to capture Lonely Trench, by men drawn from no less than four battalions, was also unsuccessful.

There could be no clearer indication of the futility of attacking well prepared and determined defenders without recourse to a wider frontage than these wasteful and ill considered attacks south of Guillemont.

The attacks made on Guillemont between 18th & end of August

The ineffectiveness of those piecemeal attacks made on 16 August determined that subsequent assaults on Guillemont should be more focused in their approach to the village's capture. On the morning of the 17th Rawlinson and Fayolle decided that the capture of the village should occupy two days, the first of which would see a parallel French assault on Angle Wood to the south of Guillemont.

It was believed that, with the French in possession of Angle Wood and the British in control of the higher ground to the south of Guillemont, it would be feasible to imagine that Guillemont would fall on the 19 August.

On the 18th the weather proved to be dull and damp. As day broke the German positions at Guillemont, southwards in the direction of Angle Wood and further north towards Ginchy, had already sustained almost twenty four hours of steady unremitting bombardment. Throughout the morning that artillery fire continued until zero hour, fixed for 2.45 pm. As the final minutes ticked away the rate of fire never altered, in the hope that such a policy would prevent the Germans anticipating the attack. Amongst the gunners who were supporting the infantry, back at Maricourt, Ralph Hamilton described the cacophony of sound with awesome precision.

'Exactly to the second hell broke loose, and thousands of guns went off at the same moment. Never have I heard anything like it, or could have imagined such noises possible. It is quite impossible to describe to people who have not experienced it. It actually hurt, and for a time I felt as if my head would burst. All talking was impossible, and the telephones were useless. After a time I retired to my telephone-pit, which we have dug 20 feet down into the solid chalk, and 30 feet in from the entrance. There matters were almost worse, the noises were not so violent, but the vibration was so great that at first I thought my heart was going to stop, from being so jolted. If one could imagine the vibration of the screw of a ship intensified a thousand times it might give some idea of my sensations.'

As the whistles blew the field artillery brought their fire back into No Man's Land, no more than one hundred yards in front of the attacking soldiers. As the men approached towards this curtain of fire the field artillery then began to lift forward in increments at the rate of fifty yards per minute. In front of Guillemont village these attacks were undertaken by the men of the 24th Division, whilst on their right, just to the south of Arrow Head Copse, the 3rd Division employed 9

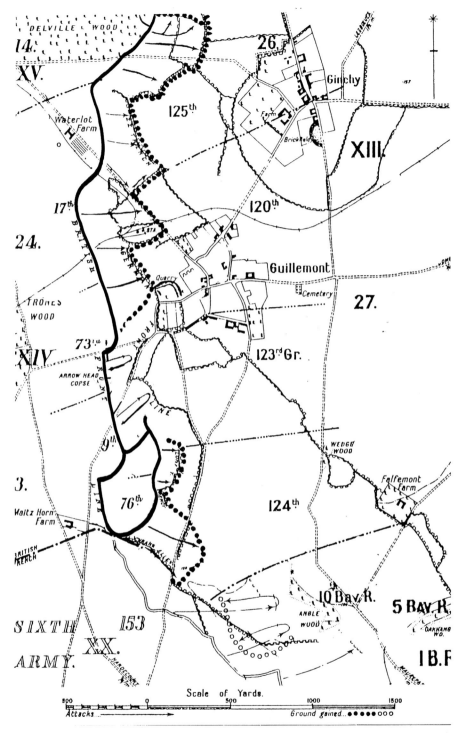

Map 10. XIV Corps attack, 18 August 1916

Brigade and then 76 Brigade in touch with the French.

In the centre of the attacks, in front of Guillemont, the troops were unable to advance their positions in the vicinity of Arrow Head and the Trones Wood – Guillemont road. A little to the north of that road some progress was made when the left hand companies of the 7th Northamptonshires managed to gain a foothold in the German lines adjacent to The Quarry (57cSW3. T.19.c.1,4). This was an extraordinary feat on the part of these men who were later reinforced by a company of the 9th Royal Sussex. As darkness fell engineers were brought forward to help in the process of consolidation here on the western outskirts of the village.

However, by far the most significant advance of the day was achieved by the men of 3rd Rifle Brigade[12] on the northern, left, side of the attack upon the village.

The Rifle Brigade's men north of The Quarry advanced with the greatest speed to take a number of German prisoners from the devastation at the Station. This battalion managed to capture a section of the Waterlot Farm road to the north-west of the station where they joined up with soldiers from the 8th Buffs who had advanced successfully into the area of ZZ Trench, west of Ginchy.[13]

On the right of the British attacks against Guillemont, in the Arrow Head Copse area and further south towards the junction with the French army, the 3rd Division employed 76 and 9 Brigade's men in attacks towards the Hardecourt road and the higher ground south of Guillemont. A segment of the Hardecourt road to the east of Cochrane Alley was captured, as was the southern part of Lonely Trench. These positions were terribly exposed and the Germans began to pour an enormous weight of artillery fire into the area, counter attacking the French who had taken ground in the Maurepas ravine. Some of the 1st Gordon Highlanders in the Lonely Trench area were forced back to maintain their right flank in contact with the Frenchmen. Nevertheless, the following morning it became clear that the Germans had themselves withdrawn to the Falfemont Farm – Wedge Wood lines. The now empty Lonely Trench was thus immediately re-occupied and the men began the consolidation of the Guillemont – Hardecourt road (in the areas 57cSW3. T.25.c and 62cNW1. B.1.a). Throughout that evening and into the night the artillery rumbled on:

'Hour after hour it went on without a second's pause. Sometimes there seemed to be a comparative lull, and then immediately it was off again worse than ever. Now at midnight we are firing much slower, a shell every minute, but there are so

many hundreds of batteries engaged that even that rate is one continuous roar. The men are very tired, and the layers nearly exhausted, although we have changed them as often as possible. My guns have already fired nearly a thousand rounds each and are red-hot. We have to keep swilling them out with our precious little stock of water. Every now and then I have to stop one gun to allow it to cool, meanwhile increasing the fire of the others.'[14]

During the night of 19/20 August the 3rd Division's frontage and part of the frontage previously occupied by the right of the 24th Division was taken over by the bantam soldiers of the 35th Division who once again found themselves facing the forbidding village of Guillemont. Early that morning whilst the bantams were settling uncomfortably into their ravaged trenches Fourth Army commander, General Rawlinson, was in conference with his corps commanders. Apart from disseminating information about the imminent arrival of the 'tanks', and the possibility of using these within a major September initiative, Rawlinson took the opportunity of making it known that he expected the western side of Guillemont to be captured the following day, 21st August. The remainder of the village would be taken three days later on the 24th, then moving forward across the spur towards Angle Wood whilst the French would capture Angle Wood and Maurepas. The British right flank unit was the 17th Lancashire Fusiliers; their operation orders make interesting reading, revealing that the battalion took over from the French 127th Regiment d'Infanterie in the Angle Wood sector, thus extending the British frontage south of Guillemont. This attack was part of the preparation required to ensure that the tanks, when their time came, could be launched from the main ridge running across the battlefield from Leuze and Bouleaux woods, past Ginchy, High Wood, Pozieres and onwards towards the east of Thiepval.

On 21 August the 35th Division were due to make two attacks opposite Guillemont. The first was at 5.00 am when they made an attempt to capture German positions opposite Arrow Head Copse. Whilst this proved unsuccessful, further north the men of the 8th Buffs and the 3rd Rifle Brigade again scored a success by taking that greater part of ZZ Trench leading into the northern part of the village. Later in the day the 35th Division's role in the attacks planned for 4.30 pm was reduced to the discharge of a smoke diversion whilst soldiers of the 24th Division effected a frontal assault on the western face of Guillemont. However, these attacks made no progress since any positions captured proved impossible to hold onto.

Hauptmann Ernst Junger and Captain F.C. Hitchcock, MC

After the war both these two officers wrote very different accounts of their experiences here at Guillemont. Junger's book, *Storm of Steel*, became a widely read classic. Hitchcock's book, *Stand To!*, never attained such distinction but is, nevertheless, an interesting and detailed account of life with an infantry battalion, the 2nd Leinsters. Both men describe evocatively the trying circumstances of battle. I have placed their accounts of the terrible shelling which occurred around the 23rd August side by side, editing these of extraneous detail.

German troops, on church parade, in the village of Combles before the events of August 1916 reduced it to a bloody and shattered shambles.
An der Somme

A British infantry battalion moving across the battlefield in platoons, advancing in support of operations to the south of Guillemont in 1916.
Taylor Library

Junger's day started with his arrival at Combles which was under the most intense and indiscriminate artillery bombardment which utterly devastated the village, killing many of the civilian population who had stayed on there, believing it to be a safe distance behind the lines. Junger caught sight of a 'little girl dead in a pool of blood on the threshold of one of the doorways'. Everywhere the sickly scent of death abounded. Ernst Junger and his men were about to relieve troops in the centre of Guillemont village. They assembled within the square and were festooned with items destined for the front line.

'Then we moved off in single file. Every man had the strictest orders to follow closely on the man in front. Next

On 23rd August, Captain Hitchcock who was serving with the 2nd Leinsters, part of 73 Brigade, 24th Division, had also been ordered to relieve a front line position that evening. He was to replace the men facing the south-western fringes of Guillemont to the right of the Trones Wood to Guillemont road, level with Arrow Head Copse. His route up to the front lines took him along the lane leading north-eastwards from Carnoy towards Montauban. Arriving in what he described as 'the Valley of Death' [Maltz Horn valley] the 2nd Leinsters came under sustained and accurate shellfire.

23rd August.....there we were with our transport all round us! Sergt. McCarthy, Transport Sergeant, gave the order to trot,

88

Ernst Junger

we were following, mostly at the double, a white band laid down over the open ground to give the direction. It was shot into small bits. Often we had to come to a halt at the worst moment, when our guide lost his way. To lie down was forbidden, in case we lost touch.

In spite of this, Nos. I and 3 platoons suddenly vanished. On again! We got to a sunken road, much shelled, where the sections stowed themselves. 'Lie down' was the order. A nauseous and oppressive scent warned us that this road had claimed many a victim. After a run that threatened death at every step we reached a second sunken road in which battle headquarters were concealed...

On and on! Some of the men collapsed as they ran, for we were compelled to force the last ounce from their exhausted bodies. Wounded men called to us on left and right from the shell-holes, and were disregarded. On and on, with our eyes fixed on the man in front, along a knee-deep trench formed of linked-up shell; holes of enormous size, where the dead were almost touching. Our feet found little purchase against their soft and yielding bodies. Even the wounded who fell by the way shared the same fate and were trodden beneath the boots of those who still hurried on.

And always this sickly smell. Even my orderly, little Schmidt, my companion in many a dangerous patrol, began to reel. At last we reached the front line. It was held by men cowering close in the shell-holes, and their dead voices trembled with joy when they heard that we were the relief. A Bavarian sergeant-major briefly handed over the sector and the Verey Light pistol.

My platoon front formed the right wing of the position held by the regiment. It consisted of a shallow sunken road which had been pounded by shells. It was

F.C. Hitchcock

and I then heard R.S.M. Smith's voice; 'This way, C Company.' He gave great assistance that night, standing out under a heavy barrage directing the companies as they came up. The men were splendid, and did not budge – just stood up with heads bent, no rushing about to look for cover. Tom Morrissey and Reid were superb, kneeling out under the barrage attending to McDonnell, who was just dying. We left them there, while Gerry Liston led the Company up the shallow C.T. on the rising ground.

The C.O. met us near Battalion Headquarters and conducted the Company across the open and behind the front line to the sunken road junction. Here we entered the trench and proceeded to take over or relieve the isolated sentry posts in our area. On arrival, we learnt that Poole and Barry, who had gone on in advance to reconnoitre the line, had been wounded. We actually relieved two units, both of which were Bantam Battalions! The umpteenth battalions of the Gloucester Regiment, and Sherwood Foresters[15]. Our men chaffed the little West Countrymen with uproarious Irish badinage. The Battalion found itself astride the sunken road with Guillemont some 150 yards away. We were in the exact line that we had held on the night 18th-19th August. A Company was on the left in front of Arrow Head Copse. We, C Company, were on the right. Both companies joined at the barrier on the sunken road where the Battalion bombers and a section of the Machine-Gun Corps were posted[16]. C Company also found a detached post away on the right flank. Later, I was to get well acquainted with this isolated detachment. B and D Companies were in support and reserve respectively. Battalion Headquarters was behind A Company and parallel with the sunken road. On duty all night, as Liston

Ernst Junger

a few hundred metres left of Guillemont and a rather shorter distance right of Bois-de-Trones. We were parted from the troops on our right, the 76th Regiment of Infantry, by a space about 500 metres wide. This space was shelled so violently that no troops could maintain themselves there.

The Bavarian sergeant-major had vanished of a sudden and I stood alone, the Verey light pistol in my hand, in the midst of an uncanny sea of shell-holes over which lay a white mist whose swathes gave it an even more oppressive and mysterious appearance. A persistent, unpleasant smell came from behind. As I had no idea how far off the enemy were, I warned my men to be ready for the worst. We all remained on guard – I spent the night with my batman and two orderlies in a hole perhaps one yard square and one yard deep.

When day dawned we were astonished to see, by degrees, what a sight surrounded us. The sunken road now appeared as nothing but a series of enormous shell-holes filled with pieces of uniform, weapons, and dead bodies. The ground all round, as far as the eye could see, was ploughed by shells. You could search in vain for one wretched blade of grass. This churned-up battlefield was ghastly. Among the living lay the dead. As we dug ourselves in we found them in layers stacked one upon the top of another. One company after another had been shoved into the drum-fire and steadily annihilated. The corpses were covered with the masses of soil turned up by the shells, and the next company advanced in the place of the fallen.

The sunken road and the ground behind was full of German dead; the ground in front of English. Arms, legs, and heads stuck out stark above the lips

F.C. Hitchcock

felt very ill, but would not leave the line. I walked all night, visiting the sentries. It rained hard, and we got shelled severely every half-hour. I rested for some time on a muddy fire step, with 8464 Corpl. Broadbent. Private O'Leary, Jim Marsland's scout of Hooge days, was standing up on the fire step on sentry-go beside me. I left them in that position, and in ten minutes returned to find a colossal shell-crater in the parapet, or where it had been. Poor Broadbent was dead, and badly smashed up, and O'Leary, the keen sentry of ten minutes previously, was terribly cut about the head and body – and was raving. Morrissey and Reid took him away – never did I expect to see him again[17]. We spent the night deepening the trench, and building up the parapets. What cover suited the Bantams of 4 feet 8 inches to 5 feet did not suit the 2nd Leinsters, averaging 5 feet 10 inches! 24th August... At 5 a.m. I met the C.O. who had come up to inspect the line. He was particularly sympathetic about the casualties. We toured the whole Company front, including the detached post. To get to it we had to cut across the open. However, as it was foggy, the Huns did not observe us. We found Jameson and his platoon under deplorable conditions, all around them were enemy dead, and the little ditch of a trench full of mud, with pieces of equipment and half-buried corpses. Jameson was cheery, but complained of being short of rations. This post on the right of the Company was at least 200 yards away from the main line. It had no C.T. or wire entanglements, but was echeloned back facing Leuze Wood. Later in the day I got in touch with the unit on Jameson's right. We were subject to heavy shell-fire all morning. C.S.M. Kerrigan got badly wounded in the arm; also Sergt. Dignam and a few men.

From Battalion Headquarters we

Ernst Junger

of the craters. In front of our miserable defences there were torn-off limbs and corpses over many of which cloaks and ground-sheets had been thrown to hide the fixed stare of their distorted features. In spite of the heat no one thought for a moment of covering them with soil. The village of Guillemont was distinguished from the landscape around it only because the shell-holes there were of a whiter colour by reason of the houses which had been ground to powder. Guillemont railway station lay in front of us. It was smashed to bits like a child's plaything...

Just before ten at night the left flank of the regimental front was heavily shelled, and after twenty minutes we came in for it too. In a brief space we were completely covered in dust and smoke, and yet most of the hits were just in front or just behind. While this hurricane was raging I went along my platoon front. The men were standing, rifle in hand, as though carved in stone, their eyes fixed on the ground in front of them. Now and then by the light of a rocket I saw the gleam of helmet after helmet, bayonet after bayonet, and I was filled with pride at commanding this handful of men that might very likely be pounded into the earth but could not be conquered. It is in such moments that the human spirit triumphs over the mightiest demonstrations of material force. The fragile body, steeled by the will, stands up to the most terrific punishment.'

After a short period in such squalid and terrifying circumstances Junger was relieved. Hours later he was wounded by shrapnel whilst at Combles. Junger was evacuated to hospital whilst his unit, the 73rd Hanovarian Fusiliers, were later reintroduced to the horrors of Guillemont. They were there on 3rd September when the village was finally captured by the soldiers of the 20th Division.

F.C. Hitchcock

understood another unit was taking over this detached post. Shell-fire was hellish all afternoon. Box barrages were put down all round, and the earth was going up like volcanoes, completely smothering us. The heat was intense, and as we were all sweating pretty freely, we got into a filthy state. Crouching in the trench, hugging the forward side, one could feel every minute small stones and lumps of earth ricochet off one's helmet. Now and then one would be almost smothered by the parapet being blown in. The dirt flying about and the fumes from the lyddite added to our discomfiture. During a bombardment one developed a craze for two things: water and cigarettes. Few could ever eat under an intense bombardment, especially on the Somme, when every now and then a shell would blow pieces of mortality, or complete bodies, which had been putrefying in No-Man's-Land slap into one's trench. Shell-fire, too, always stirred up the swarms of black flies, of which there was an absolute plague on the Somme battle-fields. The bombardment was intense, at times it reminded me of Hooge exactly one year previously. I had been in command of the Company all day, and as part of our front line on the right of the sunken road was completely obliterated and untenable, I got the platoons to side-step to the flanks. Our whole line was one cloud of smoke, evidently the Huns anticipated an attack as they sent all kinds of coloured SOS Very lights up. I got our Lewis guns into position and gave the order to fix bayonets. (In such a case this is always good for the morale.). Throughout the bombardment the men were splendid, not a sentry shirked his duty.'

Later, on the 25th, having suffered numerous casualties from the persistent shelling the 2nd Leinsters were relieved by soldiers of the 20th Division.

Wrecked rolling stock at Guillemont station.

The entire area in and around the village was littered with the putrifying corpses of British and German troops.

Once again the timetable for the capture of Guillemont had been thrown into disarray.

The instructions which Fourth Army had intended to issue relating to the 'final' capture of Guillemont on 24 August therefore had to be modified quickly. On the right it was anticipated that the French would advance the whole of their frontage north of the River Somme, and that the 35th Division would advance in step[18] – but not attack the German secondary positions. Meanwhile the 20th (Light) Division, which as we have noted had taken over from the 24th Division in front of Guillemont and south-west of Ginchy, were expected to capture the northern part of Guillemont and the German trenches on the south-west of Ginchy.

Events had overtaken the attacks planned for 24th August. Throughout 23rd and 24th the Germans persistently bombarded the British positions opposite Guillemont and Ginchy making any preparation impossible to contemplate. The utter lack of any surface water posed an enormous problem for the attacking troops. One battalion, due to attack alongside the French, knew that its men would have to stay out in exposed positions all day prior to the assault. Their records state that:

> *The water supply is a matter of great difficulty; there is no water in the line and all water has to be carried from about Brigade HQ at night. Men must therefore be warned that one bottle of water has to last them for the whole 24 hours, and must accordingly be used sparingly.*[19]

Nevertheless, during the dark early hours of August 24 the bantam soldiers of the 17th Lancashire Fusiliers in this area were able to make their assembly on the extreme right of the British frontage, across the north-east face of Angle Wood from B.2.c.4,3 to B.1.d.3,6. Well before dawn the men were concentrated in shell holes, in advance of their front lines, where they stayed concealed throughout the day. At 5.45 pm the French I Corps attacked and succeeded in getting into the German's main Second Positions south-east of Falfemont Farm, up to B.2.d.4,8 and also making good their control of Maurepas. The 17/LFs innovative assembly and concealment tactics enabled the men to advance alongside the French with few casualties, reaching the 110 metre contour at the south-western end of the Falfemont spur[20]. Falfemont Farm, with its strong defences amongst the surrounding copse and within its extensive cellars and outbuildings, was thus finally within realistic assaulting distance.

The success on the right flank was good news for Rawlinson and his

Corps commanders who were coming under increasing pressure from Haig. The Official History reports that:

'Conferring with his Corps commanders on the morning of 25th August, General Rawlinson read a GHQ letter, received the previous evening, which emphasised the extreme importance of securing Ginchy, Guillemont and Falfemont Farm without delay. The Commander-in-Chief considered the task well within the power of the troops and artillery available, providing that the higher commanders, bearing in mind the standard of training which existed among the troops and subordinate leaders, gave their personal attention to the details of preparation.' [21]

As a consequence the attacks upon Ginchy were allotted to XV Corps whilst XIV continued to pit itself against Guillemont. The 5th Division was added to XIV Corps for the attacks to be made on 29 August. However the tactical situation for the British was worsening as rain on

The objective – Guillemont village – a devasted wasteland.

the afternoon of the 25th began to turn what were already badly churned trenches into a nightmare of mud and which made the digging of new communication trenches a tortuous process. The storage of ammunition and the preservation of food and drinking water suffered accordingly. The German artillery was still very active and the British troops were now experiencing the very worst that summer weather and the German army could throw at them. As the weather worsened Haig prevailed on the French for a postponement, initially to the 30th. When the bombardment for these attacks began on the morning of 29th poor visibility made artillery observation impossible and another one day's postponement became inevitable. That afternoon a very heavy thunderstorm broke in the Somme area, causing the French to delay further - this time determining 3 September as their preferred date - although Haig and Rawlinson were in no position to argue against Foch's wishes since their own positions in front of Guillemont were in a state of considerable devastation.

31 August was the first fine day for nearly a whole week. The scene was therefore set for the final battle for Guillemont village.

1. Originally spelt as Faffemont on contemporary French maps.
2. Amongst the wounded were the battalion's commanding officer, Lieutenant Colonel A.M.Mills, and his second in command, Major Sir H.S.M.Havelock-Allan.
3. Guillemont village was bisected in an east/west manner by its main street, identified on British trench maps as 'Mount Street'. The eastern limits of the village were defined by a road running north/south. The segment of that road north of Mount Steet was therefore identified on trench maps as 'North Street' and that to the south as 'South Street'. Mount Street ran east away from Guillemont past the village communal cemetery en route towards Combles.
4. Many detachments of Bantams were attached to units within 89 Brigade to serve as carrying parties, moving forward with the 4th waves of assaulting infantry.
5. See *Manchester Pals* for more detail of this and other attacks made here by the Manchester Pals battalions.
6. A Territorial Division raised in west Lancashire.
7. High Holborn was the stretch of the Guillemont to Longueval road to the north-west of Guillemont. Brompton road was the track which ran across the northern side of the village from S.24.d.8,5 to T.19.a.8,2. Machine Gun House was located at S.24.b.7,4.
8. The 1/8th King's battalion's casualty list gives 5 officers and 10 OR killed, 8 officers and 47 ORs wounded, 502 ORs missing. The 1st King's rollcall on 2nd August counted just 120 survivors in total.
9. Churchill was not then a member of the Cabinet. His critique expressed concern about the profligate waste of life in the pursuit of minimal strategic, and even tactical, gain. This document had ben circulated to all Cabinet members during late July.
10. Chavasse Double VC. Ann Clayton. Leo Cooper, 1992. pp 161. This excellent volume details the whole extraordinary story of Noel Chavasse's life.
11. *The History of the King's Regiment (Liverpool)*. Wythall. pp 311.
12. The title 3rd Battalion of the Rifle Brigade is a rather confusing one in that the Rifle Brigade was in fact a regiment of the British Army. During the 18th August attacks on

95

Looking north-eastwards in the direction of Delville Wood from the Maltz Horn Crucifix, south-west of Guillemont, on the Hardcourt to Trones Wood road.

Guillemont the 3rd Rifle Brigade were the right hand battalion of 17 Brigade.

13. There is a very fine and now well maintained private memorial to one of the 3rd Rifle Brigade's subalterns, 2nd Lieutenant George Futvoye Marsden-Smedley, who was killed in action here on 18 August 1916.

14. *War Diary of the Master of Belhaven.* Lt.Colonel Ralph G.A. Hamilton. 1924, John Murray. Republished 1990, Wharncliffe (Pen & Sword Books, Barnsley).

15. Men of 105 Brigade, 35th (Bantam) Division.

16. NB. This is not the Trones Wood to Guillemont road but a smaller farm track, still walkable today, which ran from 57cSW3, S.30.b.9,7 to the south-west. The part of this sunken lane where the two companies met was located at S.30.b.6,0.

17. In a footnote to the original text Captain Hitchcock says that; 'Years afterwards I ran across this man whom I had believed to have died of wounds, walking across the square at Fort St. George, Madras.'!

18. On the night of 22/23 August the 35th Division had taken over Angle Wood from the French, thus extending the right of the British frontage.

19. 17th Lancashire Fusiliers' War Diary. PRO WO95/2484.

20. Later in the day the Germans launched a heavy bombardment against the 17/LF's new positions and the battalion ended the day suffering almost 100 casualties.

21. *Official History, Military Operations in France and Belgium, 1916*, Vol 2. pp 202.

The Rue d'En-Bas, Guillemont's main street, today. Compare with picture on page 49.

Chapter Five

THE BATTLES FOR GUILLEMONT VILLAGE

Part 2. September 1916 – The Battle of Guillemont

The weather during the first days of September 1916 was greatly improved. As the forward troops' trenches began to dry the men's morale improved, aided by the commencement of the British bombardment at 8.00 am on 2 September which in some way compensated for the persistent German shelling of the British forward positions; circumstances which had so drained the spirits of the British

The positions on the right of the British XIV Corps which were to be attacked by the French on the morning of 3rd September 1916. This photograph was taken looking north-eastwards across the Combles ravine (marked as Vallee de Maurepas on your IGN map). On the right is the village of Maurepas.

Above: German howitzer gun crew and below a trench mortar team operating from a dugout.

soldiers in the Longueval, Delville Wood, Ginchy and Guillemont vicinities. The British advance was planned to take place behind a rolling barrage, advancing at the rate of 50 yards per minute. The 5th Division, which was to attack on the right of the attack, issued orders that its men should keep as close as humanly possible to within 25 yards of that curtain of fire!

The objective of XIV Corps' attack was identified as a line across the north-eastern edge of Leuze Wood, a position which it was hoped would dominate and secure any subsequent attack upon the important village of Combles. The junction with the French would be within the steep sided valley or ravine south of Falfemont Farm. The plan envisaged that Falfemont Farm would be captured by the right of XIV Corps, during a preliminary attack in advance of the main assault which would begin at noon.

The preliminary attack on Falfemont Farm was undertaken by the 2nd KOSBs at 8.50 am but this gallant attempt was an utter disaster. The French, on the KOSB's right, were unable to get forward in the face of heavy machine-gun fire. To compound this problem the French artillery had been redirected away from the ravine and the attack about to be undertaken by the KOSBs, in order to deal with a German attack to the south. That redirection was never transmitted to XIV Corps HQ and the attack therefore proceeded without artillery protection. Hundreds of the KOSBs were cut down.

At 12.00 noon the attacks of 95 Brigade, 5th Division, to the south of Guillemont began. The brigade's most important task was the capture of the spur (at 57cSW3. T.25.c central) to the south of Guillemont village on the Hardecourt road. This task was entrusted to the 12th Gloucestershires on the right and the 1st Cornwall Light Infantry on the left. The men carried the German front line and then pressed on during the next stage, at 12.50 pm, to capture the German main Second Position between Wedge Wood (at 57cSW3. T.26.c.0,3) and the southern extremities of Guillemont itself. The greater proportion of the casualties incurred during this second stage of the

Falfemont farm viewed across the terrain where the 2nd KOSBs were decimated on the morning of 3 September 1916. (From 62cNW1. B.2.c.4,3 just in front of Angle Wood.)

Site of original
Falfemont Farm
(see photo on page 114)

German machine
gun fire from the
Combles Ravine
area

KOSB's direction
of attack

attack were suffered by the Gloucesters who were taken in enfilade from the Falfemont Farm positions which were still, at this stage, in German hands.

At the same time that the Gloucesters were advancing towards the north-east of Wedge Wood another attack upon the Falfemont Farm position was undertaken by the 15th and 14th Royal Warwicks. The artillery fire provided for this assault was laid down by British units, but was still described as 'feeble'. Unfortunately there were still German troops on the right flank of this attempt to get forward and their enfilade fire therefore prevented a successful British assault on Falfemont Farm. However, further to the left, the 14th Warwicks did gain a foothold in the trench just south of Wedge Wood.

Later that afternoon, at 2.50 pm, the soldiers of 95 Brigade then continued their advance eastwards and made good the Wedge Wood to Ginchy road on the rising slope to the north of Wedge Wood. During this process a large number of German prisoners were taken, notably men belonging to the 73rd Fusiliers and the 164th Regiment. As soon as the British troops could reach the top of that rise and look down upon the devastation which was Guillemont village they saw an extraordinary sight. The wreckage was now in the hands of the 20th Division's men who had finally achieved what, up until this time, had seemed an insurmountable task.

During the subsequent hours of the afternoon of 3 September 13 Brigade was replaced in the line by 15 Brigade whose attacks towards Falfemont Farm and the Wedge Wood position had mixed fortune. On the right, at Falfemont, the 1st Cheshires and 16th Warwicks were unable to get forward, again because of machine-gun fire from their right flank. However, on the left the 1st Bedfordshires reached and took Wedge Wood and made contact with 95 Brigade who now overlooked Guillemont to the north of Wedge Wood. To the men in that small wood and those dug in along the Ginchy road it seemed that German resistance east of Guillemont had collapsed. However, an advance towards Leuze Wood, the brigade's final objective, was denied on the grounds that the 20th Division's capture of Guillemont had been compromised by the failure of XV Corps to capture Ginchy at the same time. Any advance upon Leuze Wood would therefore have created a very exposed and untenable salient.

The Capture of Guillemont by the 20th Division[1]

Although the village of Guillemont retains a great deal of association with the 20th (Light) Division's success in capturing the

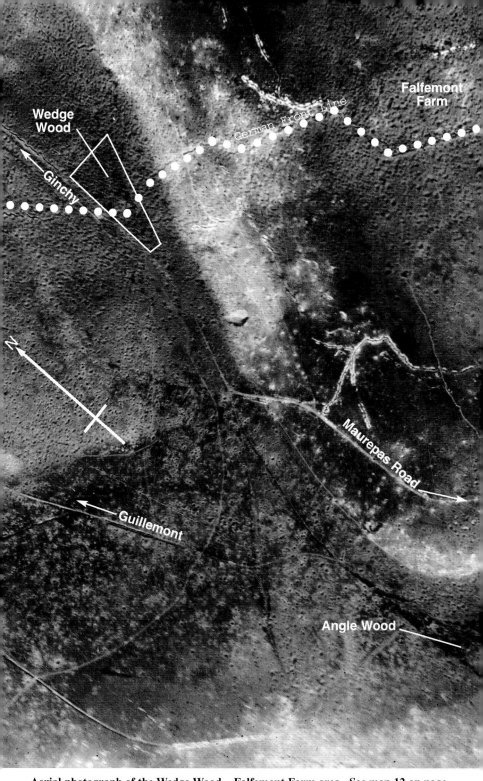

Aerial photograph of the Wedge Wood – Falfemont Farm area. See map 12 on page 115.

village on 3rd September, the division was in a parlous state on that day, even before the final attacks commenced. Casualties beforehand had already reduced the effective rifle force of 59 Brigade to just 1650 whilst 60 Brigade was so affected by sickness and casualties that its replacement by 47 Brigade, drawn from the 16th (Irish) Division, had been a necessity. The objectives set for the 20th Division's attack was the Wedge Wood to Ginchy road, east of Guillemont. In front of the British forward positions the village had been reduced to little more than a lunar landscape of interconnected shell-holes. German trenches had ceased to have any visible line, but beneath the rubble a number of deep dug-outs had withstood the shelling. Still deeper, a number of tunnels which connected the village's wells had been constructed by the troops who had been in occupation for the previous two years. These tunnels were still viable and provided the opportunity for soldiers to move safely, more than ten metres beneath the surface.

The British artillery preparation of the area was complex and thorough. As with the area south of the village attacked by 5th Division's men, the assault on Guillemont was to be made in three stages, each progressing behind a creeping barrage, that running through the village at a rate of just 25 yards every minute. A feint bombardment, fired as if to presage a British attack, occurred at 8.15 am and the area between Guillemont and Ginchy also received a special bombardment at 8.33 am. The final attack was to be made at 12 noon after a final and heavy bombardment of the German positions in front of and within the village.

The southern part of the village was the objective of 59 Brigade, and within that brigade the men of the 10th KRRC had pressed forward as close as possible to their own barrage even before zero hour at 12.00. Although casualties were thus incurred from their own artillery, the men's initiative enabled them to take the Germans by surprise. On the left of the 10th KRRC the 6th Connaught Rangers had also caught the Germans unaware by using the same tactic. The Irishmen were however more than impetuous and swept forward without putting an end to all signs of resistance in the area around the quarry, thus obliging one company of the 10th KRRC to mop up after the Irishmen in that vicinity as the morning unfolded. Moments later, at 12.00 precisely, the rest of the line advanced from their trenches and within minutes the German's front positions up to the Hardecourt road and the western end of Mount Street[2] were overrun by 59 Brigade's

Thomas Hughes VC

102

men. In the context of this action one notable distinction was won by Private Thomas Hughes of the 6th Connaught Rangers who hailed from County Monaghan, Ireland. He was awarded the Victoria Cross [*London Gazette*, 26 Oct. 1916]:

> 'Thomas Hughes, No.3/5027, Private, Connaught Rangers. For most conspicuous bravery and determination. He was wounded in an attack, but returned at once to the firing line after having his wounds dressed. Later, seeing a hostile machine gun, he dashed out in front of his company, shot the gunner, and single-handed captured the gun. Though again wounded he brought back three or four prisoners.'

His own account is as follows:

> 'On the 3rd of September we went over the top. After being hit in four different places, I noticed a machine gun firing in the German lines. So I rushed up, shot both the chaps on the gun and brought it back. I remember no more until I found myself down in the dressing station. P.S. - I forgot to mention I brought four German prisoners with the gun.'

The left flank of the 20th Division's attack was delivered in a south-easterly direction by the 7th Leinsters of 47 Brigade. These men's attack had been delivered from their assembly trenches dug adjacent to the north side of the railway line, north-east of Guillemont station and east of the road from Longueval and Waterlot Farm. The assault had been particularly successful and owed much to the courage of the battalion's bombers, who were led by Lieutenant John Vincent

Present-day view eastwards from 'the quarry', on the German main Second Position trench, looking past 'Mount Street' which ran towards the centre of Guillemont.

The Quarry

Mount Street

Site of German main Second Position

Holland. Holland was another Irishman, born in July, 1889, at Athy, County Kildare. He was educated at Clongowes Wood College, and at Liverpool University. Holland was something of an adventurer and travelled extensively in Brazil, Argentine, Chile and Bolivia, where he was engaged in ranching, railway engineering and hunting. He returned to England on the outbreak of war and enlisted in the 2nd Life Guards on 2 September 1914. He was gazetted Second Lieutenant in the 3rd Battalion Leinster Regiment, in February 1915. After arriving in France, Holland was attached to the 2nd Battalion Royal Dublin Fusiliers. He was wounded at the Second Battle of Ypres. After recovery from his wound he went back to France and was then attached to the 7th Leinsters as Battalion Bombing Officer. He then saw service at Loos, Hulluch and the Somme in 1916.

Holland was awarded the Victoria Cross [*London Gazette*, 26 Oct.1916], the citation reading as follows:

**J V Holland
VC**

'John Vincent Holland, Lieut., 3rd Battn. Leinster Regt., attached 7th Battn. Date of Act of Bravery: 3 Sept. 1916. For most conspicuous bravery during a heavy engagement when, not content with bombing hostile dug-outs within the objective, he fearlessly led his bombers through our own artillery barrage and cleared a great part of the village in front. He started out with 26 bombers and finished up with only five, after capturing some 50 prisoners. By this very gallant action he undoubtedly broke the spirit of the enemy, and thus saved us many casualties when the battalion made a further advance. He was far from well at the time, and later had to go to hospital.' [3]

It was clear to the Royal Flying Corps' observers that the German resistance in Guillemont was being overwhelmed. By 12.50 pm the advance to the second objectives began on schedule, the leading battalions of 59 Brigade now being reinforced by the 6th Oxford & Bucks Light Infantry and the 7th Somerset Light Infantry. The soldiers of the 6th Connaught Rangers were leapfrogged by the 8th Royal Munsters. These soldiers then advanced eastwards along Mount Street and began to consolidate along the line of North Street and South Street which defined the eastern perimeter of the village. To the east it was difficult to see evidence of likely German resistance and to many of the soldiers and officers on the spot it seemed that German resistance had broken down. This was one of the few occasions when signallers were able to operate without interference, allowing the divisional commanders a rare opportunity to control events without interminable delay.

View eastwards towards Leuze Wood from the site of the 20th (Light) Division's memorial.

At 2.50 the advance to the third objective, the Maurepas to Ginchy road, was made – within an almost surreal calm. In the area of 47 Brigade the 6th Royal Irish actually moved forward to the sound of

Looking towards Ginchy from the Guillemont to Combles road. This near section of the road was consolidated by the soldiers of 47 Brigade, attached to the 20th Division from the 16th (Irish) Division, by the afternoon of 3 September. Further north the 7th Division's attack had initially succeeded in entering Ginchy, only to be expelled during the afternoon's fighting.

Left: The spoils of battle – German prisoners being marched off to captivity. Above: The task before those assigned to clear up – collect, identify, bury and mark.

their battalion pipers. Brigade HQ wired 20th Division's HQ that there seemed to be 'nothing in front'. Very considerable numbers of prisoners were captured, some of whom seemed more than glad that their ordeal was over. The British captured more than 700 hundred wounded and unwounded men in the confines of Guillemont this day, the German dead lying in profusion all around the vicinity. During the afternoon the soldiers of 59 Brigade made contact with the men of 95 Brigade, 5th Division, on their right. Unfortunately it was on the left of the 20th Division, at Ginchy, where problems were emerging.

That Ginchy situation was creating much nervousness amongst the staff at 20th Division's HQ. The divisional commander, Major General W.Douglas Smith, forbade any general advance towards Leuze Wood and sent forward the 12th King's to reinforce the men of 47 Brigade astride the Ginchy to Guillemont road. As afternoon deepened two German counter attacks from the Ginchy area were repelled by machine-gun and rifle fire organised by these detachments of the 12th King's on the south-western fringes of Ginchy. Amongst these men was Sergeant David Jones whose deeds were to become the stuff of legend in his home city, Liverpool.

Newspaper reports of the action, soon made available in Liverpool, paid great tribute to Sergeant Jones' coolness and determined qualities.

'Sergt. Jones was the right man in the right place at the right moment,' was how a fellow non-commissioned officer of the Liverpool Regt. summed him up. 'We walked right into hell by the back door, and suffered terribly. All our officers bowled out. The men were like sheep without a shepherd. Things were all in a

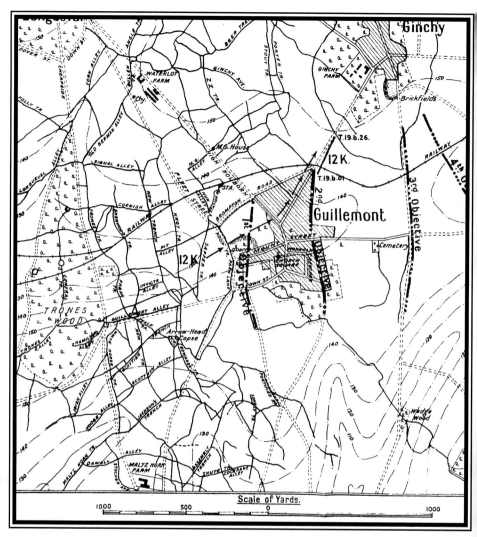

Map 11. Showing the 12th King's at Guillemont. [Taken from *The History of the King's Regiment (Liverpool)*, pp320. Everard Wythall. Pub. Arnold, London, 1930.]

muddle. Nobody seemed to know what to do. Sergeant Jones sprang forward and gave orders. The men quickly recovered their temporary dismay, and under his directions they resumed the rush on the enemy's position. The machine guns played hell with us, but the Sergeant led us straight to the goal. We carried the position with a rush, though we were greatly outnumbered. The enemy fled in panic, and we lost no time in making ourselves at home in the position. All night long the enemy deluged us with shell fire, and twice they attacked with great fury. They were determined to overwhelm us by sheer weight of numbers, but under the orders of Sergt. Jones we put our backs into it and drove off the Huns each time. We had neither food nor water, and the circumstances were about as depressing as they could be, but Jones never despaired. He was so cheerful himself that everybody felt ashamed to be anything else. So we held on like grim death for two days. We smashed the enemy up every time they tried to overwhelm us. It was very hard fighting indeed, but the boys stuck it well until relief came. We had been given up for lost. Nobody ever expected to see us again. That we had come through the ordeal safe and with honour was due entirely to Sergeant Jones's handling of the men, and nobody will begrudge him the honour he has won.'

D. Jones VC
[National Museums & Galleries on Merseyside - King's Regiment Collection]

'He ought to be an officer,' was the remark of a private who served under Sergeant Jones during the two days' siege:

'He led us with great skill, and completely baffled the foe at every turn. Nothing could dismay him. At times there was enough

Resting, near to Waterlot Farm, after the fierce fighting for the village of Guillemont.

Left: This vivid photograph of a dead British soldier was taken at Guillemont in early September 1916.

to make one's heart sink to the boots, but Sergeant Jones was as chirpy as could be, and his cheeriness was infectious. We all felt sure that nothing could go wrong with us under his leadership, and we were right.'

Sergeant David Jones, No.14951, was born on 10 January 1891. He was the son of working class parents and was educated in a local council school in Everton. Before the war he was an employee of Blakes Motor Company as an apprentice fitter. For his bravery and devotion to duty at Guillemont on the Ginchy road during the 3rd, 4th and 5th September 1916 he was awarded the Victoria Cross [*London Gazette*, 26 Oct.1916]. The citation reads:

'David Jones, No. 14951, Sergt., 12th Battn. Liverpool Regt. For most conspicuous bravery, devotion to duty, and ability displayed in the handling of his platoon. The platoon to which he belonged was ordered to a forward position, and during the advance came under heavy machine-gun fire, the officer being killed and the platoon suffering heavy losses. Sergt. Jones led forward the remainder, occupied the position, and held it for two days and two nights without food or water, until relieved. On the second day he drove back three counter-attacks, inflicting heavy losses. His coolness was most praiseworthy. It was due entirely to his resource and example that his men retained confidence and held their post."

Once Guillemont had been captured, and the lines between the 7th

The shattered trees of Trones Wood form a background to these troops in front of Guillemont.

Division in the north around Ginchy, through the 20th Division's positions east of Guillemont towards the 5th Division's men west of Falfemont Farm linked, the men began to settle for the night. It was to be a torrid experience. Just before nightfall a number of German planes overflew the area and within minutes a very accurate bombardment of the British positions was begun. Rain began to settle in as darkness shrouded the area. At 11.00 pm Rawlinson ordered that the attack should continue the following day, at 3.10 pm, and that the artillery should commence a preliminary bombardment at daybreak.

That day, 4 September, dawned damp and cool. After the customary artillery bombardment a number of important local corrections were undertaken to ensure the security of the British success at Guillemont. Valley Trench[4], north of Falfemont Farm, was captured by two companies of the 1st East Surreys. A similar detachment of men from the 1st Devons passed through Valley Trench later that afternoon en route for the near edge of Leuze Wood, which they reached at 7.30 pm, soon afterwards beginning a consolidation just inside its south-western facing perimeter.

North-east of Guillemont the situation was still shaky. The whereabouts of the 7th Division's forward troops in parts of Ginchy was uncertain, although it was clear that the Germans had considerable troop strength in the area between Ginchy village and the 'Quadrilateral' – a loop of trenches east of the village (located at 57cSW3, T.14.d.9,5.). Some patrols from the 7th Somerset LI managed to get into the western corner of Leuze Wood, joining the 1st Devon's men there, subsequently establishing a series of posts from the western corner of Leuze Wood north-westwards to the Guillemont – Combles road. However, on the left it proved impossible to make any further progress along the railway line, past the south of Ginchy towards the Quadrilateral, because of accurate sniping from the confines of the village. The day closed in miserably heavy rain.

Out in his post, south-west of Ginchy, Sergeant Jones and his group of men from the 12th King's were still exposed and hungry. They would still be there on the morrow. His regiment, the King's Liverpool, had been engaged here at Guillemont throughout all attempts to capture the village. The regiment's senior battalion, the 1st, along with its commanding officer, had been swallowed up and wiped out within the fighting. Numerous Territorial units, ordinary Service battalions and the locally raised Liverpool Pals units had all been here. The regiment's history records that:

'At a modest estimate the King's Regiment alone in the several

attempts to capture the village had losses which came near 3,000 officers and other ranks.' [5]

The capture of Falfemont Farm

As we have seen, 4 September was a day of mixed weather, windy, squally showers and alternating periods of bright sunshine. It was expected that, at 3.10 pm, the 5th Division would carry the attack past the German Second Position from Point 48[6], through Falfemont Farm and north-westwards to Wedge Wood. A subsequent advance was to be made at 6.30 pm on the Leuze Wood positions by the 5th Division's men, an objective which the 20th Division would also be seeking to reach from their positions east of Guillemont.

The attack on Falfemont Farm was made by three battalions of 15 Brigade, 5th Division. The 1st Norfolks were immediately handicapped by the inability of the French on their right to leave their trenches. The right of the 1st Norfolks was therefore devastated by machine-gun fire from the Combles ravine (Oakhanger Wood) and the

This very fine photograph shows British support troops waiting to advance from their trench near to Guillemont on 3rd September.

Present day site of Falfemont Farm

Original site of Falfemont Farm

Site of isolated graves

Falfemont Farm today. Don't be confused by the Ferme de Faffemont's location on your IGN maps, a little way south-west of Combles. The original Falfemont Farm was located within the confines of the Bois de Faffemont west of the present farm. On your trench map that location is 62cNW1, B.2.a.9,6. Falfemont Farm was thus on the German main Second Position, just south-east of Guillemont, and was surrounded by an enclosure of trees, today regrown as the Bois de Faffemont.

battalion's attacks failed. However, on the left of the 1st Norfolks one company of the 1st Cheshires managed to work their way round to the north-western face of the farm enclosure under the protection of the spur's shelter. From the north-west the 1st Bedfordshires bombed their way down the German trench, capturing many Germans who were driven towards the 1st Cheshire's men. The 1st Bedfords captured 130 prisoners, mostly from the 164th Regiment, as well as a number of machine-guns. By 4.00 pm the northern and western parts of the farm's enclosure had been captured. A further attempt to storm the farm at 5.30 pm was a failure and it was then decided that the 16th Royal Warwicks would sap towards the farm overnight. Whilst this process continued the 1st Norfolks pushed into the remaining parts of the farm not yet captured and then sent patrols to clear the area down towards Point 48 to the south-east.

Thus the positions in contact with the French were made secure and the south-eastern aspect of Guillemont could be said to be firmly held. During the period 26 August to 7 September the 5th Division's casualty lists revealed that 133 officers and 4,100 other ranks had been lost. Within the 20th Division the situation was revealed as similarly costly.

114

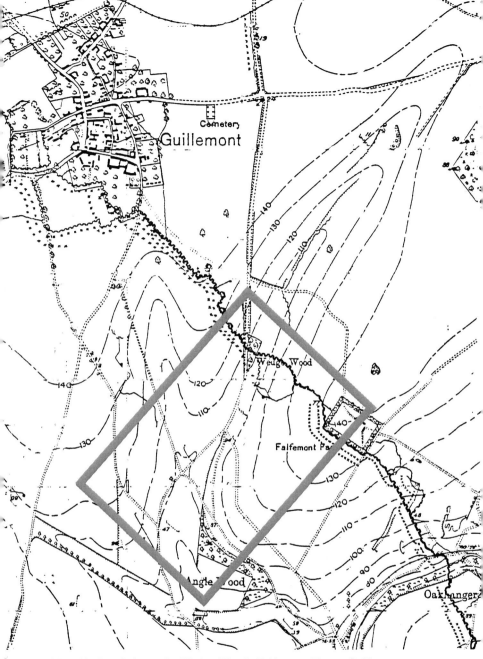

Map 12. Detail from the Wedge Wood, Falfemont Farm, Oakhanger Wood and Angle Wood areas, north of Maurepas and south-east of Guillemont, taken from two 1:10,000 trench maps which join to each other in this location. Shaded rectangle corresponds with the aerial photograph on page 101.

Between 22 August and the 8 September that division's casualty toll had mounted by 129 officers and 2,830 other ranks.

A postscript to the battles at Guillemont

The aftermath of these battles at Guillemont was the revelation of a most unspeakable concentration of death. The dead were trampled underfoot, pulverised as further units moved eastwards towards the sound of fighting at Leuze Wood and Combles. The terrain was littered with the remains of soldiers who once contested Guillemont. One man who witnessed the scene, on 4 September, was a padre serving with the 16th Division, Father William Doyle. His account of that terrible passage is a harrowing indictment of the terrible human suffering which the village beheld.

'The first part of our journey lay through a narrow trench, the floor of which consisted of deep thick mud, and the bodies of dead men trodden underfoot. It was horrible beyond description, but there was no help for it, and on the half rotten corpses of our own brave men we marched in silence, everyone busy with his own thoughts... Half an hour of this brought us out on the open into the middle of the battlefield of some days previous. The wounded, at least I hope so, had all been removed, but the dead lay there stiff and stark, with open staring eyes, just as they had fallen. Good God, such a sight! I had tried to prepare myself for this, but all I had read or pictured gave me little idea of the reality.'[7]

Sergeant David Jones of the 12th King's who had done such sterling work in rallying and commanding his detachment of soldiers on the north-east of Guillemont survived the ordeal. But David Jones' life was, almost inevitably, soon to be cut short. He was killed on 7th October 1916. Searching desperately for information, Jones' newly married wife, Elizabeth Dorothea Doyle, then inserted a number of appeals within the local Liverpool press asking for details of her husband's service career.

One officer wrote to Mrs. Jones:

'I have seen your advertisement about Sergeant Jones, V.C., in the 'Echo', and though I am not able to throw much light on the subject, I feel sure you will not mind a line of condolence and congratulation from one who has known him since November, 1914, and has therefore been able to appreciate the magnificent qualities your husband possessed. It was on active service that his merits came out so strongly. He was a wonderful scout, and

did some magnificent patrol work, which combined brain and bravery to a high degree. His fearlessness had a very great influence for good on the men of his platoon and company. Captain Ballantyne more than any other officer was able to appreciate this, being for so long his Platoon Commander. Eventually, after being a bombing officer for several months, I returned to command my own Company, and to find Sergeant Jones the Sergeant of my old platoon, No.12. I am so proud to think it was my old platoon that was with him at the time. When a Lewis Gun Sergeant became necessary, I chose him, and a better choice could not have been made. I am so proud, if very sad. And, Mrs. Jones, your great sorrow will, I am sure, be tempered by your great pride, though you will always say it would have been easier to bear if he had only known. I was in the attack on 7 Oct., and, as Senior Officer, became a little anxious as to what were the casualties. I remember asking my orderly about 8 p.m., I think, and his first words were: 'Sergeant Jones, he that did so well at Ginchy, has been killed.' I felt very cut up, as I had known him so long. Alas, many another brave man fell that day. Among them Sergt. Andy White, also in No.10, fell. But the battalion, yes, the whole Division, did wonderfully well. I know you will excuse this writing when you know my right arm is all bound up (not badly hurt), and I have to use my left hand. Mr. Fred Austin, 75, Bagot Street, Wavertree, Sign Writer, knew your husband I believe, both being connected with coach-building. He is a great friend of mine. Accept my deepest sympathy for yourself in your irreparable loss of as brave and upright a man as one could wish for.'

After the war, at his school in Heyworth Street, Sergeant Jones' bravery and sacrifice was commemorated by a marble tablet, now a part of the Museum of Liverpool Life. His was just one of the thousands of individual tragedies that went to make the extraordinary story of Guillemont. But, writing soon after the war in Germany, one other young soldier who had passed through the same storm as David Jones wrote eloquently about how the battle for Guillemont had changed his generation and all that he had thought was fine within civilised Europe.

'For I cannot too often repeat, a battle was no longer an episode that spent itself in blood and fire; it was a condition of things that dug itself in remorselessly week after week and even month after month. What was a man's life in this wilderness

whose vapour was laden with the stench of thousands upon thousands of decaying bodies? Death lay in ambush for each one in every shell-hole, merciless, and making one merciless in turn. Chivalry here took a final farewell. It had to yield to the heightened intensity of war, just as all fine and personal feeling has to yield when machinery gets the upper hand. The Europe of to-day appeared here for the first time on the field of battle.' [8]

It took a further quarter of a century before Junger's 'Europe of today' could be banished from the face of the 20th century.

1. 20th (Light) Division:

59 Brigade	**60 Brigade**	**61 Brigade**
10th K.R.R.C.	6th O&B.L.I.	7th Somerset L.I.
11th K.R.R.C.	6th K.S.L.I.	7th D.C.L.I.
10th Rifle Bgd	12th K.R.R.C.	7th K.O.Y.L.I.
11th Rifle Bgd	12th Rifle Bgd	12th King's
	Pioneers: 11th D.L.I.	

2. Mount Street was the main street in Guillemont, running east/west, that part to the east running past the village communal cemetery and thence to Combles.
3. Holland survived to become a Staff Instructor at an Officer Cadet Battalion based in North Wales.
4. Valley Trench ran from 57cSW3, T.26.c.4,0 to T.26.a.8,5. This day, 4 September, also marked the death of Corporal Edward Dwyer V.C, 1st East Surrey. Dwyer was said to have been the youngest winner of the VC when he was awarded it, at the age of only 18 years, following severe fighting at Hill 60, Ypres, during April 1915. Edward Dwyer is buried at Flat Iron Copse cemetery.
5. *The History of the King's Regiment (Liverpool)*. Wythall. pp321.
6. Located at 62cNW1, B.2.d.4,8.
7. *Father William Doyle*, S.J. A O'Rahilly. Pub: Longmans & Co. 1930.
8. Junger. *Storm of Steel*. pp 109.

After the battle; the victors of the battle for Guillemont village are taken out of the line for a rest.

CEMETERIES AND MEMORIALS

Transport and the debris of war beside the wreckage of the narrow gauge railway line, adjacent to Bernafay Wood, 1916. This is probably the original site of the cemetery to the north of Bernafay from which graves were later removed to Bernafay Wood cemetery on the west of the wood.

Chapter four

The cemeteries and memorials in this area

There are, in reality, only two cemeteries which properly fall within the scope of this guide, Bernafay Wood and Guillemont Road. In the details of the walk from Longueval to Guillemont and return via Ginchy I have also mentioned the importance of Delville Wood as the resting place of many men who were killed fighting at Guillemont during the July to September period of 1916. However, the General Tour and some of the suggestions made within this guide will lead you, of necessity, slightly outside this guide's limits and I have therefore mentioned a small number of other cemeteries which you might like to take in whilst visiting the area covered. These include Hem Farm and Longueval Road.

Bernafay Wood Cemetery

The cemetery can be reached along the D197 Maricourt to Longueval road and lies opposite the north-western face of Bernafay Wood, overlooking the upper reaches of Caterpillar Valley. A short distance along that valley to the west lies Quarry Cemetery whilst Longueval Road cemetery can be seen on the opposite, northern, side

of the valley. The cemetery provides a fine vantage point, in particular towards the site of the Dawn Attack made towards the German main Second Position on 14th July 1916.

The bare details within the register record that the wood was taken on 3 and 4 July 1916, by the 9th (Scottish) Division. On 25 March, 1918, in the retreat to the Ancre, the same Division was driven from the Wood but recaptured it for a time. On 27 August, 1918 it was finally regained by the 18th Division. The cemetery was begun by a Dressing Station in August 1916, and used as a front-line cemetery until the following April. Today Bernafay Wood cemetery contains the graves of 945 men.

By the end of hostilities Bernafay Wood cemetery originally contained 284 graves, but it was then increased by the concentration of 80 graves from Bernafay Wood North Cemetery and 558 from the battlefields immediately east of the wood facing Trones Wood. Bernafay Wood North cemetery was located opposite the north edge of the wood, a little way east of the Longueval - Maricourt road. It was begun by an Advanced Dressing Station, and used from July to October 1916. Apart from those 80 soldiers from the United Kingdom this cemetery also had the grave of one German prisoner. The great majority of the concentrated graves in Bernafay Wood cemetery, or 417 out of the whole number, are those of unidentified men. Special Memorials are erected to 9 soldiers from the United Kingdom and 2 from Australia, known or believed to be buried here as unknown; and other special memorials record the names of 12 soldiers from the United Kingdom, buried in Bemafay Wood North Cemetery, whose graves were destroyed by shell fire.

Guillemont Road Cemetery

Guillemont Road Cemetery, which during the war years was often called Trones Wood cemetery, lies between Guillemont village and Trones Wood, on the north side of the road to Montauban overlooking the very shallow upper reaches of Caterpillar Valley. Before and during the war the area just south of the cemetery was the site of Arrow Head Copse.

The cemetery register records only the briefest of summaries, saying only that the village was an important point in the German defences in July 1916, and that it was taken by the 2nd Royal Scots Fusiliers on 30 July of that year, but that the battalion was obliged to fall back; and it was again entered for a short time by the 55th (West Lancashire) Division on 8 August. On 18 August it was reached by the

The magnificent architecture of the entrance to Guillemont Road cemetery.

2nd Division, and on 3 September, during the Battle of Guillemont proper, the village was captured and cleared by the 20th (Light) Division and part of the 16th (Irish) Division. It was lost in March, 1918, but retaken on 29 August by the 18th (Eastern) and 38th (Welsh) Divisions.

Interestingly the register also mentions that the '20th Division erected a Memorial at the cross roads 450 metres east of the village; which has now been replaced by a permanent monument near the same spot'. That memorial has itself since been replaced by a further one, making the current memorial the third in succession! The register also suggests that a permanent Memorial to the 16th Division has been

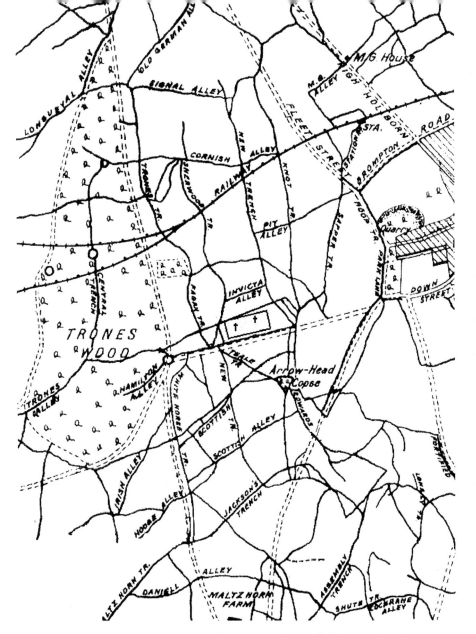

Map 13. The trenches which existed around the Guillemont Road cemetery in the late summer and autumn of 1916. As the British Army tightened its grip on the village of Guillemont the German defenders were progressively ringed with a complex network of trenches and I have given here a map which shows the location of those positions prior to the final capture of the village. The cemetery is located alongside 'Guillemont Alley' (adjacent to the Guillemont Road) and south of 'Invicta Alley'.

Guillemont Road cemetery during the late 1920s when the concentration of outlying graves into this cemetery was complete. Plot 8 is that just to the right of the entrance portal. [Garwood]

erected between Guillemont and Ginchy. However, that is now located within the village of Guillemont.

The cemetery was begun by fighting units, mainly of the Guards Division, and Field Ambulances after the Battle of Guillemont, and was closed in March, 1917. It then contained 121 burials, besides a number of regimental memorials. It was greatly increased after the Armistice by the concentration of 2,139 graves, almost all of the July – September 1916 period, from the battlefields immediately surrounding the village. It now contains the graves of 2,259 soldiers from the United Kingdom, one from Canada, one from Australia, one from South Africa and one from Newfoundland; and two German prisoners. Thirty-nine French graves have been removed to French cemeteries. The Registers record particulars of 740 War Dead. The unnamed graves in the cemetery therefore number a very high proportion, being 1,523 in total. A few other men are identified as groups but not individually. Special memorials are erected to eight soldiers from the United Kingdom, known or believed to be buried among the unnamed graves. The cemetery is very extensive in size, covering an area of 8,344 square metres. It is the third largest on the British sector of the Somme battlefield.

The only cemetery of any size from which British graves were brought to Guillemont Road cemetery was Hardecort Village French Military cemetery. The village of Hardecourt was captured by French troops on 8 July, 1916, and again by the 58th (London) and 12th (Eastern) Divisions on 28 August, 1918. Five British Artillerymen were buried by their unit in the French Military Cemetery, in the middle of the village, in September, 1916; and in 1918 the 12th Division buried in the same cemetery 14 men of the 9th Royal Fusiliers and two of the 7th Royal Sussex.

The original battlefield burials lie just inside and to the left of the cemetery entrance. In this section of the cemetery, amongst the first two rows, there are a number of well known and oft visited graves including those of 2nd Lieutenant William Stanhope Forbes – the son of a Royal Academician; Lieutenant Raymond Asquith – the Prime Minister's son and Lieutenant Honourable Edward Wyndham Tennant – the son of Barron Glenconner. Both the last two mentioned were associates of Rupert Brooke and shared their families' network of relationships as part of London high society's 'Souls'. Many of this grouping's sons were killed during the Great War. But perhaps the city whose anguish is most frequently represented amongst the multitude of headstones is Liverpool, whose King's Regiment was so closely associated with the capture of Guillemont and whose regimental badge appears so very frequently among the headstones.

Hem Farm (La Ferme at Hem-Monacu) on the banks of the Somme

The great sweeps and meanders of the River Somme provide a dramatic backcloth to a number of interesting British military cemeteries. One of the best known is at Suzanne where many of the early casualties belonging to the Liverpool and Manchester Pals of the 30th Division are buried. But at Hem-Monacu there is one small cemetery which is completely off the regular track of British visitors to the Somme battlefield area. This is a pity because the cemetery is full of interest and is well sited for a summer lunchbreak! To reach this cemetery follow the D938 Peronne road east of Maricourt until the junction with the D146 leading to Monacu. The cemetery is close to the river to the west of Hem-Monacu.

Hem Farm British Military Cemetery at Hem-Monacu.

Around the cemetery is a great deal of evidence pointing to the severity of the fighting here, both in July 1916 and during the two campaigns in 1918. The British took on this sector in January 1917 and the adjacent farm became the location for a Dressing Station. At the end of the war this was a tiny cemetery but later more than 500 graves were concentrated here.

Today there are therefore almost 600 graves, including those of two men who were the recipients of the Victoria Cross, both posthumously[1]. Many men were killed during the South African Brigade's attempts to defend the Leforest position, east of Maurepas, during the German spring advance through this area in 1918. The most frequently given date of death is 24th March. The Australian representation here is also strong, although in their cases almost invariably from the period August - September 1918.

Longueval Road Cemetery

This is also reached along the course of the D197 Maricourt to Longueval road, north of Bernafay Wood. It lies roughly two thirds of the way across the No Man's Land of 13 July 1916. On that date the British held the north of Bernafay Wood whilst the German main Second Position defences ringed the southern parts of Longueval. On the night of 13/14 July the 9th (Scottish) Division's men were assembled in forward positions in readiness for their successful assault

Longueval Road Cemetery looking towards Trones Wood on the left and Bernafay Wood to the right.

on those Second Positions. Whilst that assembly was taking place the final stages in the Battle for Trones Wood were unfolding just yards to the east. The right hand unit of the 9th Division, the 8th Black Watch, were deployed here at the site of the shrine adjacent to the present day cemetery.

In fact the men buried here are mostly drawn from the casualties incurred during the fighting east of here in the Leuze Wood – Combles area during September 1916. The explanation is that this location became the site of a Dressing Station, known as Longueval Alley or Longueval Water Point. One hundred and seventy one men were buried here, a small number being from 1918. During 1923-24 a further 49 were added, as a consequence of battlefield clearances in the Longueval area and concentration work, making a total of 220 graves.

The cemetery provides a very central location from which a number of interesting views can be obtained towards Bernafay and Trones Woods as well as Longueval, and Montauban.

Maurepas and the French National Cemetery

Within Maurepas village, easily reached from the 20th Division's memorial east of Guillemont, are two places of interest. Sited at the village green in the centre of Maurepas is the memorial to the soldiers of the 1st Regiment d'Infanterie who died whilst capturing the village in 1916. On the south eastern side of the village is one of the many large French National Cemeteries in this area, this one containing the graves of more than 3,600 Frenchmen killed during 1916. The largest of these National cemeteries in the area, indeed on the Somme, is located at Rancourt, east of Combles on the far side of the A1 motorway – Autoroute du Nord. It is just a short drive south of here to the site of the interesting but little visited British Military Cemetery at Hem-Monacu.

The CWGC isolated grave at Falfemont Farm

This lonely and infrequently visited spot lies between the site of the original Falfemont Farm (Bois de Faffemont) and its post war replacement which is now situated closer to Combles. Buried here are the bodies of Captain Richard Heumann, Sergeant Major B.Mills and Sergeant A.W.Torrance, all of the 1/2nd London battalion. When the three men were killed, on 10 September 1916 during an action close to Leuze Wood, the bodies were buried on the spot. This is right on the boundary limits of this guide but I have included a little detail here since many people will be walking this area in search of understanding

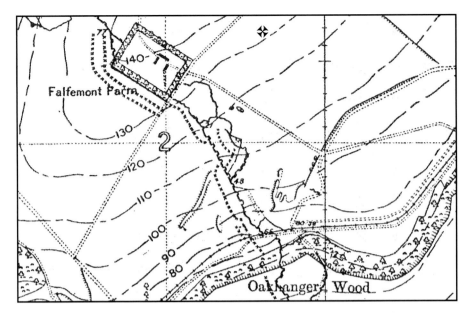

Map 14. A detail taken from the 1:10,000 trench map, 62cNW1, showing the location of Captain Heumann's grave. ✣
The present day Faffemont farm is located at B.3.a central. See photo page 114

relating to events concerned with the capture of the German main Second Positions in the Guillemont area. After the war Captain Heumann's family purchased this plot of land from the farmer, having requested that the grave not be removed to one of the ever growing concentration cemeteries elsewhere on the Somme. A stone cover was set above the grave and this, along with the border, is still maintained by the CWGC.

Captain Heumann had been Mentioned in Despatches and was described as a very popular and capable company commander. CSM Mills was the holder of the Volunteer Long Service Medal. The three men were killed whilst engaged in a company officer's conference within a shell hole. Apart from the three men buried here three further casualties were incurred from the same shell burst – Lieutenant Attenborough, Second Lieutenant Ursell and Second Lieutenant Childs who subsequently died of his wounds.

The most sensible way to get to this location is through the village of Combles. Leave the village in a south-westerly direction following the signs for the Guards Cemetery but continue past that cemetery until you reach Faffemont Farm. Although you have the right of access to what is a recognised War Grave it would be a sensible idea to ask at the farm. *'Je voudrais visiter la tombe des soldats Anglais dans votre champs, s'il vous plait'* should suffice – although I take no credit for such indifferent French! This is also an ideal opportunity to walk a small part of the German main Second Position in the vicinity of the original Falfemont Farm. The map here, a detail from 62cNW1, squares B2 and B3, should help

20th (Light) Division's memorial, east of Guillemont

This wonderfully sited memorial recalls the central part played by the division in the final capture of Guillemont in early September 1916. The original memorial commanded the ground east of Guillemont until 1993 when its stonework's deterioration could no

longer be ignored. In that year the venerable but fractured edifice was demolished and replaced with a far less vulnerable stone upon which the original bronze plaques were re-installed. The finance for the new memorial was raised and arranged through the Royal Greenjackets. The memorial was re-dedicated in 1995. Locating the site is very simple and you will be rewarded with some fine all round views from its vantage point.

The autumnal and early winter phases of the Battle of the Somme were a busy and costly period for the 20th Division. Apart from the Battle of Guillemont the division

The 20th (Light) Division's memorial east of Guillemont before subsidence and the effects of weathering necessitated that it was pulled down and rebuilt. [Thorpe]

The 20th (Light) Division memorial on the day of its rededication. [Cox]

also then took part in the Battles of Flers-Courcelette, Morval and the Transloy Ridges. The division stayed on the Somme during the bitter winter of 1916-17 until the German pull-back to the Hindenburg line in March.

16th (Irish) Division's memorial in Guillemont

The memorial was originally located on the Guillemont – Ginchy road north-east of Guillemont and commemorated the division's extensive involvement in the fighting in the Guillemont – Ginchy area. Here in Guillemont this simple stone recalls the fact that the capture of Guillemont, on 3rd September 1916, was greatly aided by the attachment of one of the 16th Division's brigades to the 20th Division. The memorial can be found adjacent to the village church.

The 18th (Eastern) Division's memorial on the south face of Trones Wood

This memorial is easily located on the side of the D64 road at the southern end of Trones Wood. The site overlooks the Maltz Horn valley and farm area to the south. It was sited here in commemoration of the sacrifice made by the 18th Division's soldiers who finally captured Trones Wood on the morning of 14th July 1916. The previous week's fighting here cost the British Army in the region of 4,000 casualties, the German Army a similar number. As with many locations on this part of the Somme battlefield the area was the scene of fighting during 1918 as well as 1916. Coincidentally it was the 18th Division again who took part in that re-capture in the September of 1918 at the start of the last 100 days of the Great War. Almost all of the 18th Division's memorials on the Western Front have the same

The 16th (Irish) Division's memorial near to Guillemont church.

characteristic shape, that of a slender pointed obelisk. This one carries the unusual phrase; 'The Greatest Thing in the World' at its base - leaving the startled onlooker to finish the sentence by his or her own appropriate words.

The 18th (Eastern) Division's memorial:
(a) Early post-war cross;
(b) Newly errected memorial in the 1920s;
(c) Present day.

Pipers at the memorial to 2nd Lieutenant Marsden-Smedley. In the background the trees of Trones Wood can be seen clearly. [Thorpe]

The private memorial to Second Lieutenant Marsden-Smedley, 3rd Rifle Brigade.

Second Lieutenant Marsden-Smedley served with the 3rd Rifle Brigade, 17 Brigade, 24th Division. He was killed, aged 19, during an attack against the Station on 18 August 1916. Apart from being an intelligent and assured young man, and belonging to his school's Officers' Training Corps, George Marsden-Smedley was an outstanding sportsman, captaining Harrow school's football and cricket teams. Had he survived the war George Marsden-Smedley would have left his home in Lea Green, Matlock, to start degree studies at Trinity College, Cambridge.

The site is best reached from the Longueval road leaving Guillemont to the north-west. The memorial is particularly poignant in that, apart from the seeming youthfulness of its focus, the inscription records that George Futvoye Marsden-Smedley fell 'and lies near here in an unknown grave. Lovely and pleasant in life – in death serene and unafraid – most blessed in remembrance.' There is another very fine memorial to this young man's memory in the form of a unique stained glass window within the church of St.John the Baptist at Dethick, Derbyshire.

Individual French private memorials

Within the southern sector of this guide that area attacked by the French during the 1916 Somme offensive has given rise to a number of individual private memorials which you will come across. All are within a short distance of each other. The first of these relates to Captain A.Cochin whose memorial is located half a kilometre along the road leading northwards out of Hardecourt towards Guillemont at a junction where a left fork diverts towards Trones Wood. The second of these memorials lies adjacent to the D146E Hardecourt to Maurepas road and is dedicated to the memory of Gaston Chomet. The third memorial, that of V.Hallard, is within the village of Maurepas. As already noted, Maurepas is the site of a substantial French National Cemetery to the south-east of that village

'Le Monument aux Soldats Francais morts le 28 Aout 1914'. This substantial stone monument, which testifies to the severity of the fighting here during the first month of the war, was photographed soon after its construction in the mid 1920s. The monument is located opposite the communal cemetery, east of Guillemont. [Reed]

1.Second Lieutenant G.E.Cates, 2nd Rifle Brigade and Private R.Mactier, 23rd Victoria Battalion, A.I.F.

Chapter Seven

Tours and Walks

This section of the guide provides a series of tours and walks. The first of these is a general tour, too long to undertake except by cycle, car or coach, designed to make you familiar with the main geographic features and sites of historic interest to be found within the area. Primarily this guide is concerned with Guillemont and the two woodlands on its western approach, Trones and Bernafay Woods. Because the area covered by this guide is extensive those of you with cycles might consider bringing them along. The locations around Guillemont certainly lend themselves well to exploration on two wheels, especially during the summer months. As a general rule of thumb a walk described as taking roughly three hours should be capable of being completed on a mountain cycle in one quarter of that time, depending entirely, of course, on how long you care to dwell at the many places of interest. The detailed walks described here will allow you to develop a more intimate understanding of the particular locations described. Whilst stopping at places of interest I suggest that you periodically cross reference with the relevant sections of historical narrative and cemetery – memorial entries.

A general tour of the area to familiarise yourself with the main features around the area covered by this guide
This tour is suitable for cars and coaches. If you stop at all the suggested locations the circuit may well take four hours to complete. I suggest that you make use of the relevant IGN maps. The Green series 1:100,000 Laon – Arras sheet will suffice, but more detail can be gleaned by making use of the Blue series 1:25,000 sheets, the one covering the Guillemont area being 2408 est, covering all areas described within this guide. However, the map below will help if you have been unable to obtain the IGN sheets.

Coming from Albert you can reach a suitable **starting point** for this tour at the **village of Fricourt.** I suggest this since Fricourt was attacked, on 1 July 1916, by the 7th Division's men which included the 20th Manchesters. From Fricourt almost all the way along the southern arm of the British sector of the battlefield that day there were thousands of men, representatives of Kitchener's New Armies, raised in the industrial towns of Manchester and Liverpool. As you pedal or **drive eastwards along the D64** you will pass through **Mametz** and **Montauban**, both villages where the association with the Manchester Pals battalions is very strong, but nowhere is that association more notable, or better recorded, than at Montauban where the initial attack

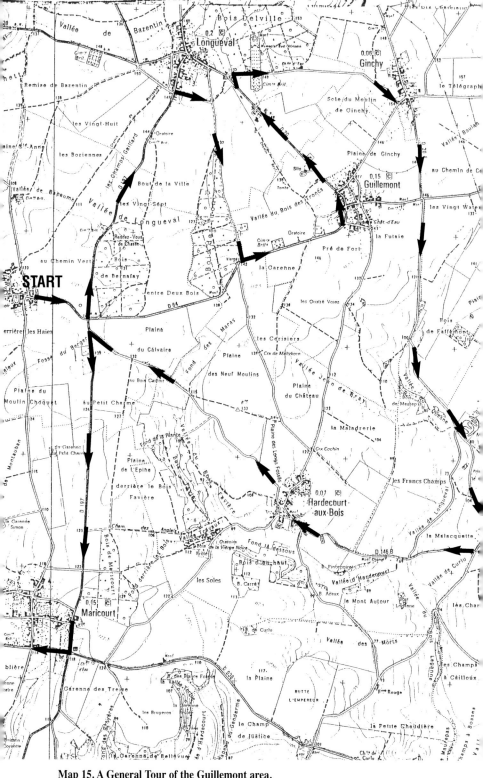

Map 15. A General Tour of the Guillemont area.

south of the village was undertaken by the Liverpool Pals (King's Regiment) and where the final capture of the village was made by units drawn form the Manchester Pals (Manchester Regiment). Within the village you will come across the very fine Portland stone memorial erected to the memory of both the Liverpool and Manchester Pals, raised there during the early 1990s. The link between the cities of Liverpool and Manchester and their Regular, Territorial and Pals battalions with the area covered by this guide continues into the two woodlands east of Montauban, Bernafay and Trones, as well as to the village of Guillemont itself. More recently the King's Regiment

The very fine memorial, dedicated to the memory of the Liverpool and Manchester Pals, which is to be found in Montauban.

(which raised the Liverpool Pals) and the Manchester Regiment have amalgamated into a unified organisation and it can be said without concern of contradiction that the King's regiment's part in the story of Guillemont is unique.

From Montauban **continue eastwards**, still on the D64, in the direction of Guillemont. You will soon come to a **cross roads** where, facing you on the front left, is Bernafay Wood. **Turn left** and travel **north** in the direction of **Longueval along the D197**. En route to Longueval you will pass along the western side of Bernafay Wood which was, at the start of the Somme battles, roughly mid-way between the German front line positions and their main Second Position. In this area the distance between the front lines and the German main Second Position was considerable and Bernafay Wood was therefore not within the British infantry's objectives on 1 July. Nevertheless, Bernafay Wood was organised for defence by the German army and a number of significant trenches had been dug, both within the wood's confines and between Bernafay and Trones Wood further east. As you approach the northern end of Bernafay you will come across Bernafay Wood military cemetery on your left. The cemetery slopes from left down to right as you look at it and those slopes lead down into the shallow depression of Caterpillar valley. **Continue along the D197** and you will pass Longueval Road British Military cemetery on your right with its relatively small number of graves. Four hundred metres **past that cemetery turn**

right, by-passing the southern end of Longueval. The village was a vital feature on the German main Second Position. The area to the west of Longueval was that attacked by the British infantry during their remarkable Dawn Attack on 14th July.

Travel for three hundred meters before turning **right again**, heading in a southerly direction towards the northern tip of Trones Wood. On your left is Waterlot Farm which was also an important location on the German main Second Positions. **Continue southwards** passing the eastern perimeter of Trones Wood on your right. Fifty metres before the small stand of trees which juts out from the eastern limits of the wood pause for a short while. This is where the two light railway lines which passed through Trones Wood emerged on its eastern perimeter. The two lines then joined and ran across the open ground at the head of Caterpillar valley towards Guillemont Station whose site is still plainly visible just to the north of that village.

At the D64 turn left along the Guillemont road, travelling past Guillemont Road Cemetery. This is a fascinating cemetery with a most impressive entrance. The cemetery slopes downwards, away to the north, and into the last eastern vestiges of Caterpillar valley's long course from Fricourt to Guillemont. As you **enter Guillemont stay to the left** and pass the church on your left, crossing straight **over at the cross roads** and heading towards Longueval **along the D20**. This will take you past the site of the Station, adjacent to the grain silo, which lies on the left of the road some 300 hundred metres past the Ginchy turnoff. Travel past the site of Waterlot Farm and then **turn right at the communal cemetery in Longueval**. This is a little outside the area covered by this guide, but the route is worthwhile in that it brings us past the South African Memorial at Delville Wood and thence into Ginchy village.

As you **enter Ginchy turn left** and **then very soon right onto the D20E**. The D20 runs due south. At the **cross roads** with the 20th (Light) Division's memorial **go straight over** and follow that sunken road and the **signs for Maurepas**. One kilometre after the cross roads you will be able to see a stand of trees on your left which is Wedge Wood. Just past Wedge Wood you can look up the slope of the Falfemont spur, to your left, towards the original site of Falfemont Farm. The area in front of you south-eastwards in the direction of Maurepas and south-westwards to Hardecourt lay within the confines of the French army's sphere of operations during the Somme battles of 1916. **Continue into Maurepas** where there is a notable and large French National military cemetery on the south-eastern side of the village. The village also provides the location for an individual and private memorial to a French soldier, V.Hallard.

From Maurepas **take the DD146E** in the direction of **Hardecourt**. En route, on the left hand side of the road, you will see another private memorial to Gaston Chomet. The village of Hardecourt is roughly two and a half kilometres south of Guillemont, lying half way between the German front line positions (located between Bois de Maricourt and Bois Faviere) and the German main Second Position in the Falfemont Farm – Maurepas area. On 1 July 1916 Hardecourt lay outside the objectives allotted to the French XX Corps north of the Somme, although the wood to the west of Hardecourt, Bois Faviere, was due to be captured as was that to the south of the village, Bois d'en Haut. In the event both woods were taken as the Frenchmen, on the right of the British 30th Division, swept forward to Curlu on the banks of the Somme by the evening of 1 July.

In Hardecourt take the Montauban road crossing the valley south of Trones and Bernafay. (In some contemporary accounts this valley is referred to as Death Valley. There were of course a number of other locations so called. The Official History refers to this valley as Maltz Horn Valley and I have used that nomenclature throughout.) The latter part of this road is a sunken lane and is that from which most of the early attacks upon Trones Wood were made. At the **junction with the D197**, just south of Bernafay Wood, **turn left** in the **direction of**

MONTAUBAN   BERNAFAY WOOD   TRONES WOOD   BOIS FAVIERE

Looking north towards Bernafay Wood from the Chemin des Anglais, north of Maricourt, which was the junction between the British and the French armies on 1 July 1916.

Maricourt. Almost immediately, on your right, is the site of the Briqueterie which was captured on 1st July by No.4 Company of the 20th King's.

The road to Maricourt is close to the junction between the British 30th Division and the French 39th Division on their right. Five hundred metres south of the Briqueterie ran the important German reserve position known as Dublin trench which was both the British and French objective for 1 July's attacks here. The German front line was roughly 1,500 metres south of the Briqueterie whilst the British – French front line facing them was level with the northern tip of Bois de Maricourt which is the large woodland area on your left as you approach the village of Maricourt. Interestingly there is a track which runs due east from the road across the tip of the Bois de Maricourt which is called the *Chemin des Anglais* [the English path].

From Maricourt **return to Albert along the D938**.

Walk One. Bernafay Wood

This is a pleasant stroll around the wood taking in the two cemeteries to the west and north. It is quite possible to complete the four kilometres of this walk in an hour and a half. A suitable **starting point is the cross roads** near the south-western corner of the wood. Just to the south of here was the site of the Briqueterie which was captured on the morning of 1 July 1916 by the 20th King's. Adjacent to the Briqueterie was Chimney Trench which connected Nord Alley with the sunken lane leading towards Hardecourt. The sunken lane just a few yards to your south was thus the easternmost and most forward position captured by the British army during the first day's fighting of the Somme offensive. Patrols from this vicinity on both 2 and 3 July revealed Bernafay Wood as empty. The wood was eventually attacked and captured at 9.00 pm on 3 July with only six casualties! The two battalions which undertook this capture at so little cost were the 6th KOSBs and the 12th Royal Scots.

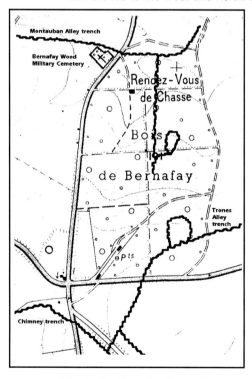

Map 16. The Bernafay Wood walk.

Leave the cross roads in a northerly direction **keeping the perimeter of Bernafay Wood on your right**. Although the wood lay between the front lines and the main German Second Position it had been organised for defence. Eight hundred metres walking will bring you to the British military cemetery west of Bernafay Wood. It is a very attractive and interestingly sited location, overlooking Caterpillar valley, marked as the Vallee de Longueval on your IGN maps, and being constructed on the site of a very important German trench known as Montauban Alley. This trench ran from Pommiers Redoubt along the high ground north of Montauban, then proceeding through the northern end of Bernafay Wood before heading northwards towards Longueval, where it was known as Longueval Alley. If you look to the west from the cemetery that is the part of Montauban Alley which was captured by the Manchester Pals on the morning of 1 July 1916.

Continue along the D197 in a northerly direction until you reach the small cemetery on your right, Longueval Road Cemetery.

Turn back to the right at the site of the crucifix and follow the track running southwards to the eastern perimeter of Bernafay Wood. As you approach the northern limit of the wood you will cross a small depression which is where one of the light railways from the west passed through this area. That line then ran across the fields on your left in the direction of Trones Wood. Those fields were the scene of reconnaissance patrols made, on the night of 3/4 July, by the 6th KOSBs and the 12th Royal Scots whose men discovered that Trones Wood was held by a number of machine-gun detachments. Whilst here it is also worth noting the unsuccessful attacks made towards Trones Wood across these fields on 8 July, by 2nd Green Howards and 2nd Wiltshires (see Chapter 3).

Continue to walk southwards down the eastern perimeter of Bernafay Wood. Three hundred metres short of the road you will find a path cut in the woods to your right. This was the site of the other light railway, this one coming from the direction of Albert past Mametz and Carnoy before passing through Bernafay Wood and then running across the open space before disappearing into the confines of Trones Wood and thence towards Guillemont. These light railways were a vital part of the Somme's economy, both before the Great War and up until the early 1960s when many were finally dismantled.

It is quite possible to walk back to the cross roads via this path through the woods. Alternatively **stay outside the perimeter** and continue to **walk towards the road**. Roughly half way between the site of the railway's exit from the wood (1:10,000 trench map reference 57cSW3, S.29.c.5,9) and the road was a very important trench known as Trones Alley which connected the south east of Bernafay with the south-western corner of Trones Wood. Along with Maltz Horn Trench the existence of Trones Alley created an important intermediate position lying between the German's Front Line and main Second

Positions. The Trones Alley trench continued within the confines of Bernafay, exiting half way along its southern boundary and thence joining up with Chimney Trench in the vicinity of the Briqueterie. **Continue walking southwards** until you reach the D64 where you should **turn right** and return to the cross-roads where we started the walk.

Walk Two. Trones Wood

This is one of the most interesting of the Somme's woodlands. It was the scene of fighting throughout the second week of the battle and from its perimeter there are a number of interesting and significant views to

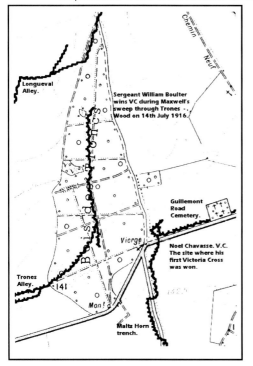

Map 17. The Trones Wood walk.

be had. The circumnavigation of the wood is approximately three kilometres and can be completed on foot comfortably within the hour. It is also possible to walk within the confines of the wood along a number of the forest rides which cut through in a north-south and east-west axis. If you intend to walk into the wood then set aside two hours.

I suggest that this walk is best commenced from the memorial at the southern end of the wood. **The memorial to the 18th (Eastern) Division stands adjacent to the D64.** Immediately behind and north of the memorial are two rides which disappear into the woodland. That on the right is the central ride and would take you almost all the way to the northern tip of the wood if you care to follow it. That on the left leads up to a small railway embankment in the western quadrant of the wood. However, at this stage I suggest that you will see much more by staying outside the wood, walking round its perimeter in a clockwise direction. It is worth noting here that immediately south of Trones Wood the land begins to fall away into the upper reaches of Maltz Horn Valley, from which direction many of the British attacks upon Trones were launched because of the relative ease by troops could approach the wood without being observed[1]. Maltz Horn Trench ran southwards along the along the road towards Hardecourt, then leading away in a south-westerly direction towards Bois Faviere.

To begin our walk **set off westwards**, briefly, along the D64 before turning **right along the wood's western boundary**. This section of the walk is rather rough and you should stay outside the boundary of the wood. On 8th August 1916 German machine gunners and artillery units firing from this western side of Trones Wood caused terrible casualties amongst the men of 2nd Green Howards and the 2nd Wiltshires. I have quoted below at length from the Official History's account of this action.

'The Allied attack, starting at 8 A.M., was to be in two stages. First the French would capture the trench, "Maltz Horn Trench", covering the knoll north of Hardecourt, whilst the British secured the continuation of this trench as far as Trones Wood and the southern half of the wood itself, "as far as the railway line". So much, it was hoped, would be accomplished by 9.45 A.M.; at an hour to be agreed upon by the divisional commanders concerned, the French would attack Hardecourt village and knoll and the British Maltz Horn Farm of which there remained only a few heaps of rubble. After some discussion Lieut.General Congreve issued an order at 8 A.M., the hour at which the first assault was to be delivered, for the completion of the capture of Trones Wood in the second stage.

The re-entrant at the junction of the two Armies presented a problem of its own. To make the attack truly "jointive", as the French desired, the British would have to advance from La Briqueterie to Maltz Horn Farm across 1,100-1,500 yards of open fire-swept ground: opposite the French, No Man's Land was only 800 yards wide. It was therefore decided to secure the southern half of Trones Wood as a preliminary operation, since part of the approach thereto from the southern part of Bernafay Wood was not exposed to view from Longueval, although it was commanded by Maltz Horn Trench. The attack on Maltz Horn farm and trench could then be made south-eastward across the shallow head of the Maltz Horn valley which was entirely hidden from the German 2nd Position.

In the early hours of the 8th the objectives were bombarded by the XIII Corps heavy artillery and the batteries of the 30th Division, the 18th Division artillery firing on the southern edge of Longueval. The 2nd Green Howards, of the 21st Brigade (Br.-General Hon. C. J. Sackville-West), which formed up for the assault behind Bernafay Wood moved through the wood at 7.15 A.M., being much impeded by fallen trees and thick undergrowth and subjected to considerable shell fire.

At 8 am the leading company, with the battalion bombers, advanced from the eastern edge, covered by the fire of the 26th Brigade (9th Division) from the left flank. The way to Trones

Wood led across a slight crest, and when they had breasted this rise the assailants were shelled by two field guns, firing over open sights, whilst machine-gun fire from the wood began to do great execution among them. The advance was checked, although attempts were made to bomb along Trones Alley and so into the wood; some men, in a gallant rush over the open, reached the edge, but they were not seen again. The Green Howards were now withdrawn, and the 2/Wiltshire was ordered to renew the attack at 10.30 am; the brigadier, however, secured a postponement until 1 pm.[2]

I suggest that you **continue to walk northwards** outside Trones' perimeter until you reach the second of the small projections on its western side, roughly half way along that side of the wood (1:10,000 trench map reference 57cSW3, S.29.b.5,9). This was the location of the southern-most light railway's entrance into the wood. It is quite possible to walk across this ride until you emerge on the eastern side of the wood, opposite Guillemont. However, for those of you with more determination I suggest keeping outside and **walking to the northernmost point of the wood**, facing the village of Longueval. This part of the walk is conducted along a definable path and reveals just why the capture of Trones was such a necessary adjunct to the success of the Dawn Attack on the Longueval – Bazentin main Second Positions on the morning of 14th July. Without the capture of Trones Wood that advance would have been dangerously enfiladed from the east by direct fire from Trones Wood. Looking from the northern tip of the wood you are just 500 metres from Waterlot Farm, the site of which can be seen in a north-easterly direction. Just to the north of Waterlot Farm you can see the cemetery at Longueval, the visitor centre and the entrance to the South African memorial within Delville Wood.

Now **turn to walk in a southerly direction** down the eastern side of Trones Wood. On your left you can see the site of the notorious Guillemont Station, eight hundred metres to the east. Just inside the wood on your right here is the scene of the action which resulted in Sergeant William Ewart Boulter being awarded the Victoria Cross for his valour on the morning of 14 July 1916. As you approach the small stand of trees which juts out from the eastern side of Trones Wood you will come across the ride from which the southernmost light railway emerged en route for Guillemont Station. It is quite possible to walk westwards into the woodland from this point (1:10,000 trench map reference 57cSW3, S.24.c.3,1) along the course of that railway line. Contemporary trench maps show Trones Wood as having a minimal defence system organised by mid May 1916 consisting of a central trench running north-south, linking up with the Trones Alley trench running between Trones and Bernafay woods. In the south-eastern corner of Trones there was a considerable strong-point at the junction between the Guillemont and Hardecourt roads. By July that pattern of defence had not been strengthened within the wood.

If you choose to walk into the wood **follow the ride for roughly 200 metres** until you come to the central ride running north-south. **Turn left** onto that ride and continue walking until you emerge from the southern perimeter of Trones Wood adjacent to the memorial from where we started. This would be a suitable location to consider the material referring to Lieutenant Colonel Maxwell in Chapter 3.

Alternatively continue to walk down the eastern perimeter until you reach the junction with the Guillemont and Hardecourt roads. From there you can look south along the upper reaches of Maltz Horn Trench and east along the Guillemont road past the British military cemetery. The quadrant between those two directions is the scene of Noel Chavasse's deeds which resulted in his being awarded the Victoria Cross. His battalion, the Liverpool Scottish, left their mark on the trench maps of this area by being responsible for digging and improving a number of trenches such as Hooge Alley and Scottish Alley in that area between Maltz Horn and Arrow Head Copse.

Walk Three. Maricourt Wood – Hardecourt – Maltz Horn – Trones and return

This is a more prolonged walk for those of you with an interest in seeing the area which was on the right flank of the British army's attacks on 1 July 1916. It is approximately seven kilometres in length, covers some open and rough terrain and is not advisable in wet or inclement conditions! I would set aside two and a half hours to complete this walk.

A suitable **starting point** would be the *Chemin des Anglais*. This was the French front line adjacent to the 30th Division's men facing Montauban north of Maricourt. The German front line opposite this location was known as Faviere Trench and a little way to the north, in their reserve position, was an important German redoubt known as Dublin Redoubt (the Lochner Werk). It was here at the Chemin des Anglais that one notable moment signifying the 'jointive' nature of the attack was played out at 7.30 am on the morning of 1 July. Here the commanding officer of the 17th King's, Lieutenant Colonel Fairfax, and his opposite number from the 153rd Regiment d'Infanterie, Commandant Le Petit, linked arms and led the attack northwards, together.

Continue walking eastwards down the valley which runs between the Bois Faviere and the smaller woodland area to the south, the Bois Brule. The western perimeter of Bois Faviere was protected by a strongly constructed trench but this was soon overrun by the Frenchmen of the 39th Division, these soldiers pushing on eastwards until they had captured the eastern side of Bois Faviere. As you walk

Map 18. The Maricourt, Hardecourt, Maltz Horn area today.

146

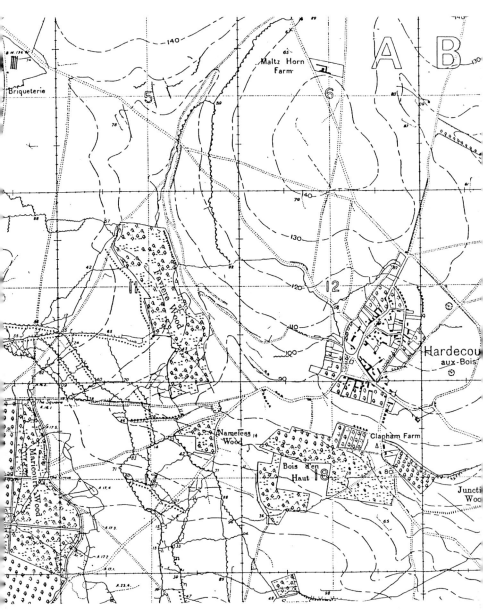

Map 19. Detail from the 1;10,000 trench map covering the Maricourt, Hardecourt and Maltz Horn Farm area, 1916.

past the southern end of Bois Faviere you will see a valley re-entrant on your left. From the north eastern end of that valley the important trench known as Maltz Horn Trench ran northwards past Maltz Horn Farm towards the south-eastern tip of Trones Wood.

Walk on into Hardecourt, keeping to the street which runs north-eastwards past the church on your right. This is the Guillemont road and half a kilometre north of the church you will come to a fork where a private French memorial, wrought in iron of florid and elaborate design, marks the death of Captain Augustin Cochin. Not far away is the simple stone marker commemorating two men belonging to the 153rd Regiment d'Infanterie, Marcel Boucher and Romeo Lapage, both of whom died here in late July 1916. Keep to the **left at this fork** and follow the rising ground up onto the high ground of the Maltz Horn plateau (the Hardecourt knoll). This location possesses one of the finest panoramic vistas on the Somme battlefield, that to the south across the French sector of the 1916 battlefield being especially extensive. Here the site of the original farm is marked by a magnificent crucifix, Calvaire de Maltzkorn on your IGN maps. This reveals the origin of the military map makers' error – the inscription commemorating the passing of this farm into history recalling that this was the site of the farm, belonging to Maltzkorn Duclercq, which was destroyed in the fighting here. Two hundred yards north of this location the Maltz Horn Trench which came up the valley on your left side (west) joined the road, then running northwards to Trones Wood. This is the location where two companies of the 2nd Wiltshires and the 19th Manchesters got up onto the French left flank during the initial attacks made on Trones Wood on 8 July 1916.

Walk down towards Trones Wood. The length of road you have just walked was that part of Maltz Horn Trench captured by the 2nd Royal Scots of 90 Brigade on 9 July. At the **junction with the Guillemont road turn left** along the southern perimeter of Trones Wood. Just before you reach the 18th Division's memorial **turn left into the fields** above the Maltz Horn Valley. This is marked on your IGN maps as a farm track but that soon peters out. It would be sensible to **fix a compass bearing due south-west** and follow that for almost **one kilometre** into Maltz Horn valley. This was the valley within which many of the 30th and 18th Division's men were moved forward along prior to the numerous attacks on Trones Wood during the period 7th – 14th July 1916. The first road which you strike will be the sunken lane running south-east from the Briqueterie towards Hardecourt.

Turn right along the sunken section in the direction of the Briqueterie, but then **first left**, some **half a kilometre before** you reach the D197, along the farm track which runs south, parallel to the D197 Maricourt – Bernafay Wood road. You can see the course of this track stretching away towards the northern tip of the Bois de Maricourt and the *Chemin des Anglais* from where we started. The important German redoubt known as the Lochner Werk (Dublin Redoubt) was astride this farm track level with the northern end of Bois Faviere. The western end of that redoubt marked the furthest advance made by the 17th King's by 8.30 am on the morning of 1 July 1916. On their right Commandant Le Petit's men were in control of the Lochner Werk and some way to the north a detachment of the 20th King's had captured the Briqueterie, but were isolated there.

One interesting postscript to this walk is one of the most impressive and well sited private memorials on the whole of the Somme battlefield, located within a kilometre of the eastern side of Maricourt on the D938 Peronne road. The granite memorial is dedicated to the memory of Lieutenant Robert Brodv, 224th Regiment d'Infanterie. His memorial is still maintained in good condition, and lies within the ground over which the men of the French 11th Division attacked on the morning of 1st July 1916. To the south there are very fine views over the Somme and down to Curlu and Hem-Monacu where there is a very infrequently visited British cemetery.

Walk Four. Longueval to Guillemont, returning via Ginchy

This is an opportunity to walk along the German trenches which formed their main Second Position north of Guillemont. It will take perhaps an hour and a half to complete, being just four kilometres in length, but full of interest. The most interesting aspect of this walk is the way in which it reveals the care which was taken to provide a panoramic field of fire for the machine-gunners whose positions were in or near to these main Second Position trenches. It is also revealing of just how closely the post-war reconstruction, fortunately for us, followed the pre-war layout in this area.

Start at the communal cemetery, looking down the D20 from Longueval towards Guillemont. Before the battles for Guillemont altered the layout of the original trench system here, the German's main Second Position lay on the south-western side of the road looking towards Trones Wood. As you walk along towards the site of Waterlot Farm you can imagine the belts of barbed wire on you right hand side. Waterlot Farm was never a working 'farm' as such. Before the Great War this was the location of a suger beet refinery, and was rebuilt for the same purpose afterwards. By the 1990s it had long since ceased to function and the derelict buildings had become a seemingly ever present eyesore in the area between Longueval and Guillemont. Fortunately these crumbling and grim main buildings were demolished in the mid 1990s.

Half way to Waterlot Farm the switch line running from Trones Wood entered the trench by the road's side. At the far end of the site of

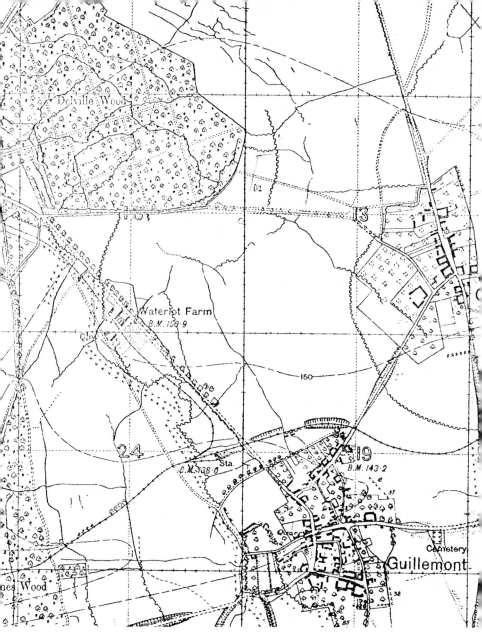

**Map 20. Detail from the 1:10,000 trench map, dated corrected to
15/8/1916, 57cSW3, showing the captured German positions at Delville
Wood (Longueval), north Guillemont and Ginchy. Note the switch line
trench (which came from the north-east of Bernafay) which runs from the
northern end of Trones into the main Second Position north-west of
Waterlot Farm. To the west of Trones Wood this trench was known as
Longueval Alley and it was a continuation of Montauban Alley trench.**

150

Waterlot Farm, on the right of the road, a **track turns off to the right** and you should **follow** this for a short distance before turning left. This track, marked as Le Chemin Neuf on your IGN maps and which was identified on the British trench maps as 'Fleet Street', will take you southwards, for a short distance along the exact site of the German main Second Position trenches. As you approach the site of the Station, on your left by the silo, you will see the private memorial dedicated to the memory of nineteen year old Second Lieutenant George Futvoye Marsden-Smedley, 3rd Rifle Brigade, who was killed in action here on 18th August 1916. The memorial is located to the Trones Wood side of the track where the light railway line approached the barbed wire entanglements in front of the German trenches here. Before the war George Marsden-Smedley had been a student at Harrow where he had captained the cricket and football teams, being described by his teachers as an outstanding sportsman. The young man had only joined the 3rd Rifle Brigade as a newly drafted subaltern in July, only to be killed here at Guillemont during his first terrible taste of action one month later. Tragically George's body was never identified and he is commemorated at Thiepval, although four of his companion subalterns who were killed with him were recovered and are buried at Delville Wood cemetery. The inscription on the memorial is one particularly revealing of the sense of tragic loss felt by his family. Also noteworthy are the great efforts which have been made to maintain and restore this memorial in very recent years.

Before the final capture of Guillemont the British had constructed a series of assembly trenches in very forward positions which lay both to the north-east of the station as well as to its south-west in the direction of Arrow Head Copse. It was from the trenches north-east of the station that Lieutenant John Vincent Holland, 3rd Battalion, Leinster Regiment, attached to the 7th Battalion, set forth with his team of bombers on 3 September to win his Victoria Cross within the confines of Guillemont.

Continue to walk past the site of 2nd Lieutenant Marsden-Smedley's memorial in a south-easterly direction, moving across the shallow depression in front of Guillemont where a track on your left was identified on the trench maps as the Brompton Road until you come to the site of The Quarry on your right. This location was part of the main Second Position and was the scene of hand to hand fighting on a number of occasions during the early attempts to capture the village on 30 July, both the 8/9 and 18 August as well as the village's final capture on 3 September! On that day this location was the scene of Thomas Hughes' gallantry which brought him the award of the Victoria Cross.

Just past the Quarry turn left. This track will lead you into the centre of the village along the street referred to on the relevant trench maps as Mount Street. A short detour from Mount Street is absolutely essential. **Turn right** and walk down to the village church. Adjacent is a simple memorial dedicated to the memory and sacrifice of the 16th

(Irish) Division's soldiers, here at Guillemont, during the final hours of its capture. East of the church at the south-eastern end of the village is a small pasture where dug-outs can still be seen. Interestingly their entrances were built to the north, suggesting that the Germans rather misjudged the way in which the battles here were likely to develop. **Return** to Mount Street and follow its course through the village, past the communal cemetery on your right. The 20th (Light) Division's memorial at the cross roads was an imposing structure. During the post Second World War years it had begun to show the ravages of time and its structure was crumbling. However, re-structuring work, carried out during 1995, has restored this well sited memorial to health and in a form less likely to require expensive maintenance in the foreseeable future.

At the **cross roads** on the Ginchy – Maurepas road by the 20th Division's memorial **turn left**, northwards, **along the D20E** in the direction of Ginchy. This road, looking southwards in the direction of Wedge Wood and for a short distance northwards in the direction of Ginchy, was the furthest point reached during the attacks made on 3 September which finally made good the capture of Guillemont village. Three hundred metres north of the cross roads, as you walk towards Ginchy, you will come to the point where the light railway crossed the road en-route towards Combles. From here the British line of advance on 3 September ran back to the west then swinging north-west around the western side of Ginchy. If you look to the north-west, across the sunken lane which leads from Guillemont to Ginchy, you will see the area within which Sergeant David Jones of the 12th King's commanded his detachment of machine gunners so determinedly during those three

One of two entrances to a German dugout near to the centre of Guillemont village. This was later used by the British during both 1916 and 1918.

days without food or water during the period 3-6 September, and which led to the award of his Victoria Cross.

You have now passed the north-eastern limits of this guide. However, your return to Longueval will take you into the most fascinating surroundings of Delville Wood. **At the cross roads within Ginchy turn left and then righ**t after a further one hundred and fifty metres to **take the road back to Longueval.** This will lead you past Delville Wood Cemetery, the South African memorial in Delville Wood and the visitor centre adjacent to that memorial. In summer the visitor centre is perpetually busy. It boasts an excellent small bookshop, toilet facilities and a cafe which would provide an admirable place to rest your feet awhile after this walk. These facilities mean that many people are drawn here and you will often have the chance to speak with visitors from all over the globe who find the interest and appeal of the Somme irresistible. The Delville Wood cemetery is not a battlefield cemetery but was created entirely by the process of concentrating graves from outlying smaller burial grounds. It is therefore worth noting that many bodies recovered from the Guillemont battlefield were concentrated during the immediate post war years into this cemetery. I have not identified a separate section in this guide to deal with Delville Wood, since the location is outside the limits of this text, but you should note that Delville Wood cemetery is the third largest on the British part of the Somme battlefield, containing more than 5,500 graves, 65 per cent of which are unknown[3]. Of those that are identified almost every man was killed in the period late July, August and September when the fighting at Guillemont was at its height. Those of you who have come to find the grave of an antecedent are most likely to find the graves of men killed at Guillemont here in Delville Wood, or at Guillemont Road Cemetery, the bulk of which is also a concentration of graves made in the immediate post war years.

1. See Chapter 3 of this guide for an outline of the attacks upon Trones Wood made during the period 8th - 14th July inclusive. Many of those attacks centred around the Manchester Pals' involvement and that is discussed at length within my book *Manchester Pals*, Leo Cooper / Pen & Sword Books, 1994. The Liverpool Pals (King's Regiment) involvement as part of the 30th Division is covered in Graham Maddocks' book, *Liverpool Pals*, Leo Cooper / Pen & Sword Books, 1991.
2. *Official History. Military Operations in France and Belgium. 1916.* Vol 2. pp 37-38.
3. The second largest cemetery is Caterpillar Valley, containing a handful more graves that Delville Wood. The largest is Serre Road Number 2.

APPENDIX

German Maps

Somme Nord. II Teil. Die Brennpunkte Der Schlacht. Im Juli 1916. Oldenburg
I.D. Berlin 1927. Courtesy of Ralph Whitehead.

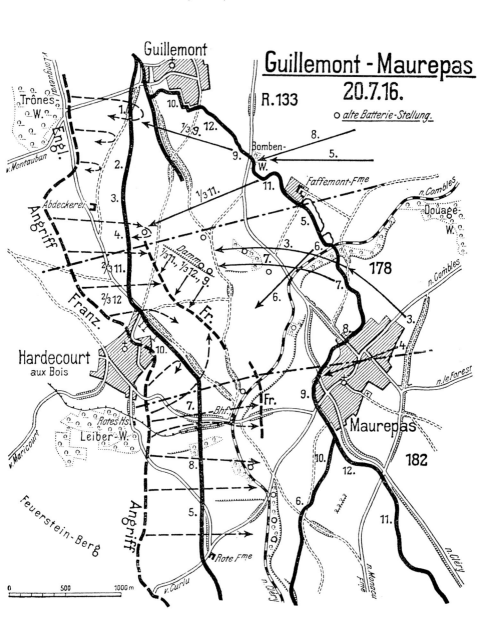

154

Guillemont-Maurepas

30.7.1916.

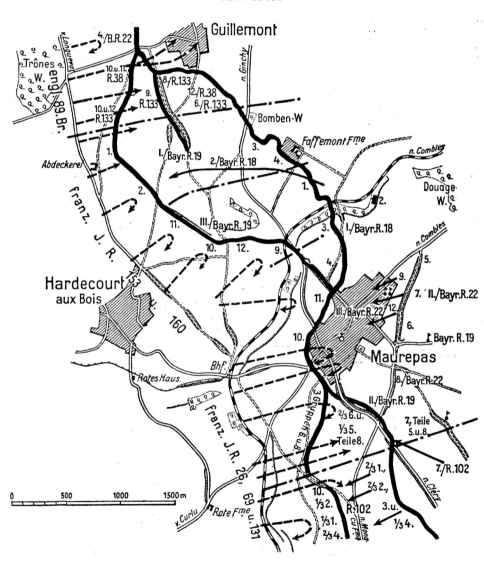

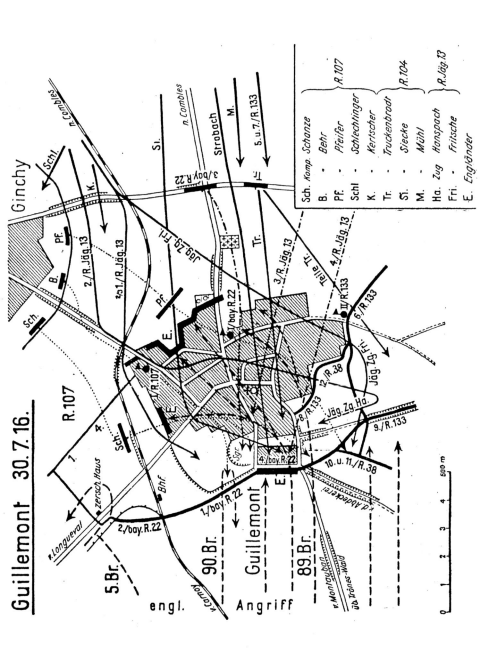

Guillemont 30.7.16.

INDEX